A SECRET CODE FOR WOMEN

IN THE BEDROOM,

BOARDROOM AND BEYOND

DISCIPLINE

SUZANNE POOL

Discipline

First published in 2020 by

Panoma Press Ltd
48 St Vincent Drive, St Albans, Herts, AL1 5SJ, UK
info@panomapress.com
www.panomapress.com

Book layout by Neil Coe.

978-1-784529-25-3

The right of Suzanne Pool to be identified as the author of this work has been asserted in accordance with sections 77 and 78 of the Copyright, Designs and Patents Act 1988.

A CIP catalogue record for this book is available from the British Library.

This book is available online and in bookstores.

Dedication

I dedicate this book to my parents, Tony and Julie, to whom I was very tough, but who loved me unconditionally – even when I didn't think they did! And to my brother, Ralph, whom I love more than he knows. Finally – to Bubs – I hope this inspires you to be all that you can be.

With love Suz x

ACKNOWLEDGMENTS

To my amazing book writing coach, Mindy Gibbins-Klein, and her team at Panoma Press, thank you for putting up with me and my procrastination. I finally got the point of my own message, and here we are.

To Marcus Bell, Peaches Udoma, and the participants of the Wealth and Impact Bootcamp – thank you for giving me the space to think and realize what I was actually up to.

To Mary Thorp, Patricia Balderrama-Garcia, Darby Fazekas, Christine Gallagher, Joanna Grimmond. Miranda McCroskey, Joanne Morton, and Kristen Moeller for your insight, support and contribution – look... I did it.

To my family – you know who you are, and you know I love you. Thank you for putting up with me all my life.

You can find out more about the content of this book on my website www.suzannepool.com. Check it out now.

You can also let me know how you feel after reading at all-eyes.suzannepool.com

Testimonials

'I felt empowered, sassy in the best way and truly motivated.'

Christine, business owner and marketing goddess

'Suzanne's straight to the point writing style is exactly what I need to hear.'

Joanne, business owner

'After the first three chapters, I am engaged in thinking about the design of my own life.'

Mary, retiree and visionary

'Just edgy enough to push me out of my comfort zone and great concepts for examining my life.'

Darby, consultant and business owner

'I felt invigorated and contemplative after I read your book. Your real life stories illustrated universal points and translated to my life.'

Miranda, lawyer

'I am left with a call to action and the experience of being empowered having read this book.'

Brittany, cancer research scientist and musician

Contents

Introduction

Hello! Thank you for picking up my book. You have demonstrated a good degree of courage and curiosity in doing so. The title alone is enough to turn many people off buying the book, let alone actually opening it up and reading it. I want you to know that I am honored that you have done so. I appreciate your time, your trust, but mostly, I respect your commitment to yourself. Buying a book called *Discipline*, and then actually starting the journey of reading it is an act of courage and a profound act of self-love. Well done. I am humbled.

I should issue you a warning at this stage. This book is not for the faint of heart. I use graphic language. A lot. It does have a purpose; it is designed to shock you and to wake you up. That is one of the key messages of the book, that you need to wake up, become aware of what's really going on with and around you, and have a look under the carpet (it might be quite smelly, so have a clothes pin handy!). But if you are in any way squeamish or a bit girly about someone using the C-word, the P-word or dropping the F-bomb, then I say this, thanks for buying the book, maybe you can find someone in your life that you think might be able to cope with it and please do them the service of gifting it to them. I will not be offended. Quite the opposite, I appreciate your honesty and acknowledge your self-awareness. You're cool with me.

This tome has the structure of an enquiry. It is an enquiry into your life, your business, your bedroom, and everything in between. I ask you to engage in a pretty rigorous examination of yourself. And I do that from the very outset. It's a worthy exercise. In finding out who you are, what you want, and how you want to make that happen, you will create your life the way that you want. You may stop relating to yourself as a victim, operating at the mercy and hands of third parties. You may stop seeking solutions and answers from other people. You may start to become your own best friend, and you may find a new level of trust and confidence in yourself. Possibly for the first time in your life.

How do I know? And how come I am qualified to say that? Because that's what happened to me; it also happened to my clients. I tell my story all the way through the book. That is the story of how and why I became a record company lawyer – the story of my difficult relationships and the story of my yo-yoing weight, among others. Sometimes there are even photos. I tell my story (rather than the stories of my clients) because I have done this work too, and first. Now here I am, the published author of this book. See what happens when you ask yourself these questions? And you engage in the thinking? You have no idea what might be possible for you after reading this book and doing this work. Go to it!

Periodically through the book, I ask you to get in touch with me. I mean that – I really want to hear from you. I really want to know how you are doing. I truly want to read what you are creating, what you discovered, and what has made a difference for you – and how it has made a difference. So, when I ask you to let me know how you're doing, please don't skip over that part. Reach out. I'm all eyes, ready and waiting – you can contact me at all-eyes. suzannepool.com. And if you really want some help, let me know that too – help!coachmenow.suzannepool.com.

One final note: there are lots of exercises dotted throughout the book; do yourself a favor – have a journal handy. Ideally a journal that you are just starting and one that you select, with love, for this purpose. You may want to keep it forever, so invest some love and thought into the journal that you use. It's an act of self-love for you... and no one else.

OK good. Got your journal and a pen? Ready to go? Good... Let's begin.

With love and gratitude for you and your time.

Suzanne x

CHAPTER ONE

YOU CAN HAVE ANYTHING YOU WANT

You can have anything you want. It's a bold statement to start the first chapter of the book with… don't you agree? Yes, it is. And it's true. Anything. Everything. All of it. Your brain may well be telling you to put this book down already. It's dangerous to make such a bold statement so early on in proceedings. And yet… you're still reading. And I'm still writing. I genuinely believe that you CAN have anything you want – you can experience anything you want to experience; you can be ANYTHING you want to be – the world is, quite literally, your oyster. So, when I suggest that you can have, experience, do, or be anything that you want, what comes up for you? Are you already cynical? Already a "yeah, but" or "um… no", or worse still, "you can say that for yourself, but that's not how it is for me." Do any of these feel, sound, look familiar? They do for me. I was there.

I truly wanted to believe that anything is possible – but life told me otherwise. I was a worldly-wise, erudite, clever and highly educated, very rational lawyer. I understood how people worked. I knew that some things were possible, but not everything. I knew that if I worked really, really, really hard, maybe some things would work out for me, but not really the stuff that truly mattered to me.

And yet, here I am writing the first chapter in this book all about how you can have ANYTHING you want. So somewhere, along the line of my (very non-linear) life, my mind got changed. And… maybe… just maybe – yours will be too. So, keep reading and let's see how we get on. How come I gave up my highly rational, and well thought out perspective that some things were possible, but not everything. That's an interesting story that, and if the truth be told, is a good place for us to begin our journey together.

I grew up in London; I was born in the City of London – within the sound of those Bow Bells that make me a true cockney, no less. I was educated at one of the finest educational establishments that the world, let alone the United Kingdom, has to offer, and life had been kind to me. I worked in the music industry, hung out with pop stars, and generally had a lot of fun. But… I was fat, I was unfit, I was single, and well… I was lonely and feeling quite stuck. I had a tricky relationship with my mother. She was proud of me; I'd done well at school (clearly), I had a good job, and I had a mortgage all before I was 30. But I was now over 30, with no husband and no sign of any of those grandchildren she wanted on the way either. I felt like something of a yo-yo with her. She would encourage me to go out and live my life, to make her proud of me, and then two weeks later she would call me and say she hadn't seen me recently and that I was neglecting my family. I was in a no-win situation.

What's this got to do with believing that anything is possible, you may be asking. Give me a minute, I'm about to get to the punchline. "I was in a no-win situation," I said a moment ago. Only that wasn't the reality. I thought I had a really good take on things, and many people, including my expensive, well-qualified therapist, agreed with me. My mother was overbearing and dominating. She was difficult and swung like a large pendulum between rejecting me and smothering me. Except that wasn't really how it was. And it was only after I realized that I was the one that was making up this ENTIRELY FICTITIOUS story about my mother that things started to alter. I had made up things about my mother and our relationship that I had neither evidence nor any actual grounds for such a belief. I had just simply decided this is how things are with her.

And so it was with my view that "Anything Is Possible." I had simply decided that there is no basis in fact for you can have anything you want. When I started to notice how fixed I had been about my mother, I noticed where I could release my view of her, and perhaps allow a different one to come into the picture. This massively altered my relationship with her. I started to realize that if I didn't believe something was possible, it wasn't because evidence said so; it was because I had a fixed way of looking at it.

Do you have fixed ways of looking at things? Do you see your husband as x, y, and z? He's never going to be the sexy George Clooney lookalike you hoped he'd become over 50. Do you have fixed ways of looking at yourself? You can't lose weight; you're never going to get promoted; you have to put your children, your husband, your parents, his parents, the dog, the cat, and everything else that there is to do and handle in life first, before you can even think about taking a bath, let alone maybe going away for the weekend with just you and a friend, or just you. You can't remember the last time you had an orgasm. In fact, orgasm... what's that? Your employees don't do what they're told; the business is never going to be as big as you envisioned it to be, and goddamn, it's soooooo much work. Those fixed ways of looking at things are what stop you realizing that the universe has your back. I have your back. YOU HAVE YOUR BACK and you CAN have anything that you want. But you have to be willing to let go of those fixations you've got and look to see what might be around them.

So... let's get started, shall we? Here's your first exercise, and since I start as I mean to go on... get your beautiful, carefully chosen journal out, and I'm going to INSIST that you do this work. This is a book about discipline – so start off right.

In your journal… tell your story. Write everything that you can think of. All the drama, the trauma, the bullying, the upset, the victories, the romance, the petty annoyances, the triumphs, and the holidays. All of it. Everything. Include in this exercise all those judgments and complaints that you have about yourself, your husband, your children, your wider family, the business people around you, and the world itself. Write down all of it – everything you think about God if you believe, or whatever your spiritual thinking and feeling. Put it all down there. Start your journal and record yourself talking – just to get a better flavor for yourself of exactly what you think and feel. Go on then… do it…

Now have a read. Read it out loud if you want. But read it. What do you notice about it? What can you see? How do you feel? Is it real? Is it reality? Is it "true?" We'll get into truth in a moment – the truth is that actually there is no truth. We just live in a society that tells us there should be truth. Yeah, that ain't happening. We all see the world through our own lens, and your lens is different from mine. Nothing is true; it's all just a matter of perception.

But back to you – so if it's all just a matter of perception, what does that tell you? It might well tell you that everything you just wrote down is, in fact, made up. None of it is real. None of it is right. So, here's a radical suggestion, given that you've just written that down in the book – rip the page or pages out – and BURN THEM. Yes, you read that correctly – burn them. It's a kinesthetic experience that will unleash something for you. Give it a go. While you're about it, when you've done that, why don't you message me and let me know how that went for you – all-eyes. suzannepool.com – or come find me on Instagram and/ or Facebook. I'd really love to hear what happened after you burned your story to a crisp.

So now that you've let go of the story and literally burned it to the ground, there's nothing right? YES, that's it, there's nothing. And that's the point; you're actually free. You let go of all the baggage that you'd been carrying for Lord knows how long. And now you can really get to work. So, let's have a look at the belief in "You can have anything you want." Anything you want… big statement as we know. But here's the crux of the matter – what do YOU want? What do you WANT? Have you ever actually sat down and thought about it? You may have had the passing thought as you've been in your favorite store, or John Lewis, or Target, both of which seem to sell everything in the entire world… I want those Apple Air pods. Or I want those Kurt Geiger shoes. (I've never actually said I want a pair of Kurt Geiger shoes, I'm more likely to want a pair of Christian Louboutin's, but you get my point.) The point is – what do you want? Do you even know what you want?

Sometimes, it's hard to know what we want for dinner! Let alone what we want for life. But that's the point; you have got to know where you are heading. Know what direction you're going in to really believe that you can have anything you want. Have you heard about the plane that was flying from Los Angeles to New York but ended up in Miami? No…! Of course, you haven't – it's never happened (unless diverted VERY deliberately) because pilots, and captains of ships, and drivers of cars, and climbers of Everest have direction – they know where they're going. They know what they want! So, YOU got to find out what you want. And by the way, this applies equally to the bedroom and the boardroom, and the kitchen, and the gym, and your husband, and your children, and well... every flipping thing really.

Let's find out what's going to give you that screaming orgasm you've been longing for – or the profit number on your P&L that's eluded you ever since you started your business. You're going to do a few fun exercises now. Time to get your journal out again...

Yes, you're going to write some lists – but good lists, not boring old grocery lists. Here's the first one: let's look at where you've been and what you've enjoyed and has given you MASSIVE satisfaction in your life already. Write a list of the top experiences in your life. All of them, every single one (if it's fewer than 100 you're not trying hard enough). Bring your discipline – do this work properly. And while you're about it, paint a picture; make those experiences vivid, shiny, like you can see, hear, feel, touch, and taste them RIGHT NOW.

Phew... that was fun – right? You probably have a giant experience of all the magic moments you've lived in your life. And that's YOUR life, not someone else's. Not Jennifer Aniston's, not Oprah Winfrey's. It's yours. Amazing! Soak that up, juice it up. And while we're about it, let's anchor that in for you. So, stand up, really tall while you're reading this, and bring those memories to the forefront of your mind – picture them, make it really colorful and bright. Feel the feelings, smell the smells, hear the sounds. And then clench one of your fists and feel those feelings and experiences lodge themselves in your fist. Juice it up! Make it bigger… Keep going. Keep going… Keep going… Yes – that's it. OK, WELL DONE! Now come back to me, and let's get on with the next part…

You've got to know where you're going and what you want. So… do you have a set of goals? And I don't mean I'd like to lose 10lbs by Christmas, or I want to get that promotion that I can see coming down the track. I mean BIG, HAIRY, JUICY, EXCITING, MAKE YOUR PUSSY WET WITH EXCITEMENT GOALS… And yes, I did just write, "make your pussy wet with excitement" – us women, we feel things in our cunts. I'm not afraid of the word cunt; it has been bastardized by men. Cunt is an old Anglo-Saxon word that describes the very sensitive part of our female anatomy – so I'm reclaiming the word for us women. Women – we feel things in our cunts. We give birth through our cunts. Life is formed in our cunts… Let's create YOUR life and feel it arising in your cunt.

Give yourself an hour – take a quiet moment now, put a timer on your phone, but put your phone on Do Not Disturb mode. Tell (yes, TELL) your husband to take the kids out for a walk in the park. And let's create your top 100 goals and experiences for your life. Speculate wildly. You want to fuck like a wild thing and scream at the top of your lungs in the Royal Suite at the Dorchester. You want to climb Mount Aconcagua. You want to own and operate an empire that makes Donald Trump's look like the size of his (very small) hands. You want to... you want to... you want, you want, you want.

Dream, it's OK. Fantasize – that's even better. Speculate, speculate, speculate. And just like you did with the top experiences of your life, make these wants and desires big, bold, beautiful, and sexy. Make them vivid, make them loud, touch them, feel them, embody them, smell them, collage them, put music to them. Do whatever works for you. But do it. Dream it. Fantasize on it. If you want to go and pleasure yourself (my editor wouldn't let me write wank), do it – it will help, but more of that part later. And if you really want the full benefit of this exercise and my support, send me pictures of what you create, send me the lists of goals. 100 of them – OK? No fewer, no more. 100! You've got the page address, but just in case you forgot – it's all-eyes.suzannepool.com

Wow. OK, I'm a bit knackered after that – but that's the case, isn't it, after a good bit of fucking (cos that's what you just did, mental masturbation, and maybe not just mental) – we're all a bit knackered. Let's just have a breath and take a moment to appreciate how far you've already come!

Look, you've burned the fiction that was the story that you were telling yourself about life. You've created a space of nothing... and then – you've filled that up with the top 100 experiences of your life, and then you've filled it up even more by fantasizing and designing the top 100 experiences that YOU WANT for your life.

Now the universe can start to do its work. But only… if you let it. Are you ready? Are you ready to put your oxygen mask on first? Are you ready to get yourself out of the way? Are you ready to make yourself the most important person in your life? Are you ready to look at someone and think, "wow, they could be like this" rather than, "they are like that?" I think that you are. But only you know that you are…

So, before we move on to chapter 2, I've got one last exercise for you to complete: write down 100 I ams. I am this, I am that. They can be bitchy, brave, brilliant. Whatever works for you. They can be empowering, disempowering, anything and everything is welcome here. I just want you to write down everything "I am" about you. 1, 2, 3… GO!

So how come I said the universe can do its work? Well, because actually, I know. You see, it was only after I started doing these exercises that I really believed that the universe had my back. Back in 2017, I was dealing with some pretty hairy shit. My father had died. My brother had come to live in my apartment because we had to sell the family home that he was living in. I had been laid off (made redundant) from my job at the end of 2016, so I was also unemployed, and life looked uncertain and uncomfortable. And suddenly, I had a windfall in my bank account that was unexpected, but entirely as I needed right at that very moment in time. About a week later, my bank called me and offered me two FREE VIP tickets to the BRIT Awards at the O2 Arena. That was the weirdest thing, actually – I had worked in the music industry for more than five years, and in all that time, I had been invited to the BRIT Awards once. And I hadn't been able to go. It had like, literally, driven me crazy as all around me, my colleagues would bang on about how great they were and how awesome the after-parties had been.

And it was my BANK that was taking me to the BRIT Awards, more than 10 years after I had last worked in the music industry. Um, excuse me? And that's what I mean; you don't know what's going to happen. You have to keep the faith and let the unexpected come. Because cum it does (and I am very deliberate in my use of language once again). You've gone a long way to making that possible – you've done the exercises in this chapter, and you've kept reading all the way through. WELL DONE! Give yourself a great big slap on the back. Why? Because this is the toughest chapter, it's the one with the meatiest exercises. It requires the most commitment from you and the most discipline to complete the work. And it also goes a flipping massively long way to getting you out of your own bloody way and allowing the universe to do its magical mistressy work. So that's that... and now... THIS.

CHAPTER TWO

THE ONLY THING STOPPING YOU... IS YOU

When was the last time you made a decision? I don't mean whether to put sugar in your coffee or not or what to have for dinner tonight. I mean an actual real-life, get your BIG girl pants on, hair-raising decision. Like quitting your job, saying yes to marrying him, what to do in your brand-new business. Have you actually ever made a decision? It's entirely possible that you will not have done. Yes, you may be married; yes, you may have left your job; and yes, you may have a successful business. In fact, all three of those things may be true about you, dear reader.

But here's the thing: did you actually decide to make any of those things happen? Or were they a bit more accidental than that? You may be saying, how is it accidental to say yes to my husband? Or perhaps it wasn't much of an accident in your mind to have started your business. And I commend you for that. But when you really get down to it, you perhaps said yes because you didn't know of a better option than the one right in front of you; and with your business, well, if the truth be told, you did actually kind of fall into it. Am I right?

Yes, I thought so. And you know what, honestly, there's no shame with that. It's pretty human actually and entirely reasonable to go through life making as few decisions as possible. But the thing is… when you do that, who's actually in charge of your life? Is it you? Or is it some other random force in the sky?

But the fact is that you are reading this book, and in fact, you've done some pretty tough self-enquiry. I got you to work hard in Chapter One, and you're still here. So even though it's pretty common, and human of you, to be in a position where really some unknown force is in control of your life, the option for you is not that. If it were, you would not have done the work that you have already done, and you would not have gotten this far in this book. That requires… discipline.

So, what to do about this conundrum of who is in control of your life. Well, here is a good place to start. Start with making a declaration. Yes – a declaration. Of independence, if you will. Today is your very own Independence Day. Congratulations. Does that mean you are going to up and leave your husband? Are you going to work on Monday (or tomorrow, depending on what day it is) with an "I quit" letter readily signed to give to your boss? Does it mean you are going to pack up and wander the earth for a year now? Well, maybe. But actually, probably not. It more than likely means that you are actually going to examine what there is in your life and decide that you want to keep it and that you are going to own it! Yes! You are going to own the shit out of your life!

And when I say own the shit out of your life, what does that actually mean? Well, before I embark on a very long-winded explanation, I want to ask you something first. How did that notion make you feel? Are you excited? Are you apprehensive? Are you running for the hills? Let's take a look first, shall we? Now I know that you dealt with your stories about the past in the last chapter, but this part bears repeating here, and you never know, it might show up again as you work your way through the rest of the book too!

The bottom line is this – declarations have power. They are a matter of your word. I will come to the importance of your word later in the book, but just trust me, declarations have power. On July 3, 1776, the United States of America did not exist; it was an idea that had not yet found its time. It was being articulated in the writings of Benjamin Franklin and others, but it was nothing. It had no existence; it was merely a thought. On July 4, 1776, with the signing of the DECLARATION of Independence, the United States of America took form. It became real. Similarly, with a marriage. As you stand in front of whoever conducts your marriage ceremony, you remain a single person – UNTIL the point at which the celebrant DECLARES (in front of witnesses) "I now DECLARE you husband and wife, wife and wife, or husband and husband (select your appropriate device)."

There are two key elements here that you should take note of:

1. There is an active declaration of something coming into existence.

2. The declaration is made publicly.

These elements are important as you consider making a declaration. Very simply put, the universe will support you once you have made a declaration – I know it sounds a bit woo woo and like the (now discredited) *The Secret*. But actually, this part of *The Secret* was accurate. Thoughts do indeed become things – when you articulate the empowering thought as A DECLARATION! and you make that declaration public, people knowing about your declaration also moves it. The universe supports this for the simple reason that Einstein said so! Energy = mass x lightspeed[2]. Yes, the theory of relativity applies here. The universe rewards and supports movement, direction, and commitment. All of which are embodied in the act of making a declaration.

Got it? Good. Go on then – let's do another exercise while we're about it. Let's have another look at those top 100 experiences you are dreaming about. You want to keep that list handy as you read through this book. It's gold that list. Which one or several of those experiences are you ready to stick a pin in and say yes, I'd like to give that one a go? I'm willing to stick my neck out and see what happens if I take that action... Write a few of them in your journal, on a new page, no more than five, and ideally around three.

Thanks for that. Now back to my lecture! One of the things that may have prevented you from making a declaration of any sort in the past is fear. Am I right? Fear that you would do the wrong thing. Fear that what you wanted to happen wouldn't happen. Fear of looking stupid and other people thinking you'd made a big bad boo boo. It's understandable really. That's our natural inclination in life. We're programed that way – be careful, be cautious, what if, what if, what if…? The trouble with that is, it stops us going for what we want.

It is us telling ourselves that we can't, we don't deserve, we shouldn't. It's fair to say it's not only us – we are programed to think that way by our educators, our parents, and the societies in which we live. Problem is it also stops us... It is a limit for us in what is possible. It has us believe that there are wrong things and right things, there is good and bad. The reality of that is NO. There is no wrong or right; there isn't any good or bad. There is merely what is and what is not. All of this right and wrong, good and bad, this or that, is merely a matter of perception – usually perception given to us by others, or inherited. Generally speaking, all of this dualist thinking is unoriginal and not actually ours.

Complicated? OK, let me explain. Yes, there are mistakes, yes, there are decisions that we take that sometimes do not work out quite the way we hoped they would or expected them to. They are merely that − mistakes. They are not failures; WE are not failures. YOU ARE NOT A FAILURE because you made a mistake. You made a mistake, move on. Take the feedback and learn. That is what mistakes are, an opportunity to learn and try something different next time.

Churchill is quoted as saying, "Success is going from failure to failure with no loss of enthusiasm." I think that sums up the point well, albeit the other point to take on board is that you actually have to take ACTION to experience what could be termed "a failure." So, let's give up the fear of taking action and that action all going a bit "Pete Tong" (which is "wrong" in British), right now, shall we?

Let's get you off that fence that's giving you splinters, and let's get you moving! One of the best ways that I have found to get you moving in the direction that you might need to go is to practice yoga. I'm going to write a lot more throughout the book about the truly life-enhancing experience of practicing yoga. For right now, I'm just going to say this: being flexible and adaptable inside of making public declarations, and giving up your beliefs about right and wrong, good and bad, will really make things a lot easier for you. It's a discipline for sure; it truly involves giving up all the thinking that you have probably been schooled with for your entire life. But trust me when I say that flexibility is a godsend and getting on the mat and practicing a triangle pose (Trikonasana) or a Warrior

II (Virabhadrasana II) is going to make a big difference for you in experiencing flexibility and adaptability in your life.

Suzanne Demonstrating Trikonasana (Triangle) Pose
©Becky Rui 2020

Suzanne Demonstrating Virabhadrasana II (Warrior II) Pose
© Becky Rui 2020

How come flexibility and adaptability make such a difference in life? Now that is a good question. Again, I'm going to say a lot more about flexibility and adaptability later on. Flexibility and adaptability are actually worthy of their own chapter. But let's just say this here and now: it gives you a much more intense orgasm, and it makes your life in the boardroom and the negotiation a lot simpler, more fun and efficient – so hear me out when I say that flexibility and adaptability will make a big difference to your life.

Being flexible and adaptable, and speaking your truth and making bold declarations is good, but it is not the complete answer to you being the barrier to your own fulfillment and success. You have to actively get yourself out of your own way. As I have mentioned a few times already, the universe rewards action; the universe is truly in your favor and has your back. But only if you do too. Energy (which is the universe) is like a river; it flows. We have this notion that energy is something we can switch on and off and generate or not. This is somewhat the case – think of electricity, we have switches on outlets to stop the current. But if you leave the switch on, the current is always there – the energy of electricity is always flowing UNLESS you actively stop it. It's the same with water – the river only stops flowing when we dam it, or we deplete the resource, but even then, nature supports us with rain, and the river starts to flow again. Universal energy and lifeforce work in the same way. You are the friction that stops you accomplishing what you want in the world. Huh? Yes, it took me a long time to get my head around this one too.

In fact, I used to yell at people when they said that to me. And they did... frequently. What the fuck do you mean, "Get yourself out of your way?" Shut up, shut up, shut up, I would yell back at them. Not in myself realizing that the, "shut up, shut up, shut up," and the yelling were in fact what was causing me the problem, and was the actual demonstration of my being in my own way. Anger and frustration are two of the most common damming emotions that we humans use against ourselves. They are literally like the rocks that stop the river. That was why I had you write your story AND THEN BURN IT so early on in the reading of this book. Hopefully, that burning of your story helped you dissipate a lot of those angry emotions that you might have felt before you started reading. Anger, sadness, fear, hurt, and guilt are the most common emotions that we humans experience that stop us accomplishing our dreams and enjoying the fulfillment and fun in life that is possible for us.

The other major rock that we like to cling on to are those limiting beliefs that we have about ourselves – I don't deserve it, I'm not worth it, I'm stupid, I'm useless, I'm nothing, and all the myriad variations that exist on top of these very gnarly and degenerative thoughts that we carry around about ourselves. Honestly, they're insidious. They're these nasty "little" things that we tell ourselves, and shout at ourselves, without even realizing it. They sit in our unconscious minds and nag away at us, our self-esteem, our motivation, and our ability to focus on what we are really committed to.

Which brings me nicely to a key reason that I wrote this book and called it *Discipline*; one of the things that being disciplined does really amazingly is have you notice your own thinking. You start to notice the excuses that you make up for yourself about how you've got too much to do, or it won't hurt if you just have one, or really – are you going to suffer if you skip your workout this once. When you have discipline with yourself, you start to notice those insidious little thought patterns and squash them like the malaria carrying mosquitoes that they really are. I understand it sounds contrary and possibly somewhat harsh. You have to be disciplined with yourself. And yes, you do, but it's the point of the book, and honestly, it's a key to having the success that you're looking for in the boardroom, the screaming orgasms you want in the bedroom, and everything else.

Here's the other benefit of being disciplined: you start to notice what your insidious thought patterns are, and you can discern how real they are (CLUE: they are not, they are entirely made up), then you can also begin to train yourself in the habit of noticing and putting to one side, noticing and putting to one side; eventually, miraculously, life alters, and you find you do not even engage in this insidious disempowering thinking that you had been so mired in for years. You hold yourself differently; you hold your abilities and capacities differently – and hey presto! You have taken yourself out of your own way. No one ever said it was going to be easy, in fact, quite the opposite. Discipline requires commitment, and quite often, it requires an experience of being decidedly unpopular and not part of the crowd. But if you really wanted to be part of the crowd and just like the Joneses up the road, I doubt you would even have picked up this book to read, let alone actually read it!

Let us take a very quick look at an area of life that may be of importance to you – there's a direct reference to it in the title of the book, so I am almost certain it's of importance to you – your intimate life with your partner, or your lack of one if you're single. Would you mind if I am direct with you? I am not a big fan of calling sex "your intimate life" – it's your sex life. Let's call it that, OK?

So… how you do sex is how you do everything… Simples. Are you telling yourself that you're not sexy? Your husband doesn't fancy you. You haven't got time for sex. You're too tired for sex. Sex is grubby and sweaty, and honestly, you can't be bothered. I don't know what all the fuss about sex is. I wasn't even that interested in sex when I was young and hot – I'm just totally over it now. It hurts, it's painful, and it takes too long. Any of this sound or feel familiar? I imagine so. Thing is, it's not just sex, is it? If you take a long hard (pardon the pun) look at yourself, you can see, can't you – those are the thoughts you have about life in general, in one form or another? Yes, the words are not quite the same, but the emotions are the same, the feelings that you have are the same, the thoughts are the same; and the general lethargy of life, well – that's the same.

Michelangelo said of carving the statue David that for him, it was a spiritual experience. He saw David inside the marble, and his actions as the sculptor were to chip away everything that was there that was not David. That's what you're doing with your life – that's what discipline provides for you in your being, bed, body, and business. You're articulating and crafting your very own work of art, with your life and YOU as the masterpiece. All those stories that you burned during the first chapter, and now those disempowering, insidious thoughts that you have about yourself – they are all the excess marble that Michelangelo is chipping away at. And in case you are wondering who the Michelangelo is in this scenario, fret not, it's not me. It's YOU.

Time to put that shit to one side, get your big girl pants on (you know, the ones you were yearning for when you were 11 and saw the high school kids strutting their stuff), and get your discipline on. Message received? Good – crack on love.

CHAPTER THREE

YOU HAVE TO OWN IT

It almost seems like it should go without saying. Of course, you have to own it. Question is, what is the "it" you have to own? And that's the key, isn't it really. This book is about discipline — the main theme, in case you had not worked it out yet, is that being disciplined and being disciplined (consider that there are two different meanings of those same two words, depending on context) will enable you to live the life you are seeking and empower you to go forth in your life as you determine. You bet your ass this is the case. But again, what is the "it" that you have to own? Well… what have we been looking at for the previous two chapters? YOU! That's right; you have to own yourself. You have to be clear about what matters to you, what's important to you, what your priorities are.

Up to this point, we have already looked at the stories that you were telling yourself about your past. We have already looked at the gnarly little limiting beliefs and decisions that you were holding on to and did not even realize. This is the insidious little (not so little, but I like to minimize them in language) baggage that we carry around during the course of our lives without even realizing it. This is the shit that stops us owning who we are and dominating our lives and businesses in the way that we want to. It's the shit that we use to gaslight ourselves with, let alone allowing anyone else to gaslight us with it. We victimize ourselves, and we completely disempower ourselves. Have I said enough? Yes, good, STOP IT. STOP IT NOW. STOP DOING THAT TO YOURSELF. INSTEAD, STEP UP, STEP OUT AND GO FORWARD.

Let's start at the beginning with stepping up, stepping out and going forward. The most important, in my mind, is learning to protect your energy and your boundaries. You are worthy of protection. You are worthy of being looked after. You are worthy. But you are not going to be protected externally, and you are not going to be looked after by other people, you may be, but do not expect it. Learn to protect yourself and take care of yourself. Now, when I say learn to protect yourself, I do not mean live in fear and dread and protect yourself from pain and hurt. Quite the opposite (as you will discover later in the book), taking risks and being willing to stretch yourself is the juice of life. But do so with mindfulness and attention to what is important and a priority for you. That is what I mean by protecting your energy and your boundaries.

Have you spent time discerning what is important to you? Do you even know what discernment means? Go and look it up in the dictionary. It's virtuous, doing work like that. Investigation and curiosity are forgotten skills and virtues about which I will say more later. Anyway, basically, I'm asking you to ask yourself some questions – like you did in the first two chapters, but this time from a more positive place. So, go grab that top 100 experiences list I asked you to create and let us work with that. You discerned that list. It isn't random. You sat and thought consciously about what it is that you want to experience, and that's what you've written on your life. That's discernment – in other words, it is about bringing conscious thought and awareness to our desires in life.

It might be the first time in your life that you have actually given consideration to what YOU want and what's important to YOU. Alongside your top 100 experiences, do you have a code of conduct and ethics? Probably not. Mostly, particularly in the West, we go through life fairly myopically, sleeping, waking, eating, going to work, working, coming home, eating, watching TV, sleeping, rinse and repeat. While there is nothing (and I really mean NOTHING) wrong with that, it's quite ordinary, and after several years of repetition is actually quite boring. Discernment is an access to getting past your boredom. And a code of conduct and ethics is a great tool in that process. Let me be very clear here though, this is a tool for you. It's not for anyone else. The code of conduct and ethics is for how YOU choose to operate in your life and the ethics by which you choose to live. These codes are

NOT ways for you to beat up on people for not living up to your standards. These codes are NOT ways for you to exert judgment over people. These codes are NOT a mechanism for you to expect people to operate; they don't know that this is your code of ethics. Am I clear? Yes, good! Go create your code of conduct and ethics for yourself – here are some questions to ask yourself as you do that:

- How do I want to be treated?

- How do I want to treat people?

- What words do I use to feel good about myself?

- What words do I use to express joy and love for myself and others?

- What words sum up the experience I am seeking in my top 100 experiences?

- What makes me feel accomplished and successful in life?

Some words that you might identify with here include: gratitude, beauty, wealth, health, love, generosity, community, grace, service, authenticity, related, oneness, whole, fun, free, fulfilled.

You might feel deeply moved or connected to yourself after you complete this exercise. If you do, that's great, hold that feeling in your left hand fist (it is an anchor point) and increase the power of the image for yourself by bringing it closer to you, making it brighter, adding sounds, smell and taste, making it sharper and bigger…

Done that? Great job! If you don't feel that way, or you feel some other way, or even you feel nothing, that is totally OK too. Just trust yourself that having completed this exercise, you have discerned a lot about yourself that you did not previously know. You may want to honor the space that you just created for yourself and create a visual artwork with your code of conduct and ethics, something that you can treasure and keep. I would love to hear from you about what you articulate in your code of conduct and ethics, so why not drop me a line to all-eyes.suzannepool. com. Or join my free Facebook community, Unleash Your Inner Vixen, and introduce yourself and post your code of conduct there, if you want to.

With your code of conduct and ethics in mind, you can consider protecting your energy and the boundaries more available to you. You have the power to focus on what's super important to you. You have the ability to create who you are in the world, based on a solid foundation of your own thinking. We live in a world where we are told that our personalities are prescribed – you are like this, they are like that, I am this MBTI personality type, the Enneagram says I am that number. OK, well as valid as all that is, it's not actually the case. Yes, you have an intrinsic personality, and some character traits that are distinctly you – some you may love about yourself, some that you find faintly shameful or unpleasant – but they are not actually fixed or attached to you. We articulate that they are, but we have the ability and capacity to create ourselves whichever way we want and desire. You have just taken a massive step forward in the process of creating yourself as you desire to be. Your code of conduct and ethics is a visible declaration (remember that?) of who you want to be and are in the world. WELL DONE! Now you can focus on bringing it forth.

Focus is important here; have you ever heard the phrase where focus goes energy flows? Maybe you have, maybe you have not. But where energy flows, heat and power are manifested in that arena, and transformation and transmutation (more about this shortly) becomes possible. Have you ever seen a blacksmith creating a horseshoe or a steelworks working on iron? That focus and application of heat enables the hard iron ore to be manipulated into something new – the horseshoe or whatever is being crafted in the steelworks. So, we're going to start applying some heat to your code of conduct and ethics and bringing some focus to what is important to you.

You may notice that as a result of your code of conduct and ethics that the tonality and timbre of your relationships have altered. You have a much more sharply focused view of what is important to you. You have a much clearer vision and articulation of how you want your life to be and who you want to be in your life. You have the power to DOMINATE your life and your business – you are putting yourself in the driving seat of your life. You are putting your own oxygen mask on first. Is it time to start saying no more often? I understand that can be troubling and uncomfortable. Are there people that you have around you that gaslight you? In other words, they undermine who you know yourself to be. Do they undermine your capacity to create your version of you in the world? Do you have the experience that they steal and suck your energy? Just say no to them − take them out of your life. You have the POWER! You can dominate your space. Yes, it takes discipline, yes they may not like you very much, but if you feel like they steal and suck your energy, if you feel like they disempower and undermine you, why the fuck do you want them in your life anyway? GET THEM OUT!

Make an inventory of your relationships − write a list of the people that you spend the most time with and occupy most of your brain space. Now take a look at those names on the page − are those relationships optimal for your life? Or do you experience them as sub-optimal (however sub-optimal looks for you)? What is sub-optimal about the relationship? Be specific − and then let's consider what you want to do about that. If it's nothing, that's totally fine, as long as you are aware that that is down to you and your choices. If it is something, what is the something that you want to do? OK, go do it!

I know this is a challenging exercise, believe me, I've been there. One of the sub-optimal relationships for me was with my own mother, as I have previously mentioned. She has been gone now for ten years, but it was (and still is) a very challenging relationship for me. I have only realized recently, with the help of that expensive therapist I mentioned, that actually she found me to be difficult, and that was at the root of our problem. SHE could not handle that I would challenge her or that I had a mind of my own. We used to butt heads A LOT, and I would often feel like I was a yo-yo around her.

Interestingly, I did a lot of yo-yo dieting while she was alive. Since she's been gone that yo-yoing has mostly stopped; in fact, in the last three years prior to writing this book, I've actually lost 90lbs in weight, through consistent, committed action and discipline (one of the reasons I feel qualified to be able to write this thing!). But the point is this: it's only once I started to address and confront the reality of my troubling relationship with my mother that I was able to heal and create some emotional distance from that, which has enabled me to live a much more effective life.

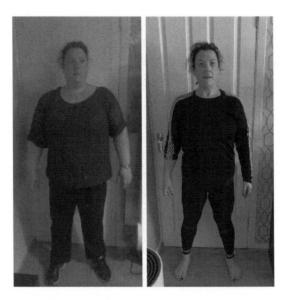

Suzanne in 2016 - left © Suzanne Pool 2016,
and 2019 - right © Caroline Rose 2019

Suzanne in 2017 © Ann Wilson 2017

So do the uncomfortable work – it's where the juice and power of who you are resides. Stretch yourself and enquire into the relationships that are working for you and the relationships that are not. Then let the people that you do not want in your life anymore know… YOU'RE DUMPED… if you want to – you don't have to, you can just more gently take them out of your equation.

You may also notice here that I am (very) deliberate with the language that I use in articulating what it is that I am seeking to communicate to you. I was, in a former life, a lawyer. On one level, choosing specific words and being careful in my articulation is a skill I have cultivated over years… and years. On another though, I am selectively demonstrating something to you and have been throughout the book. In the matter of owning your shit, your life, your business, your body, all of it, the words that you choose are critical. I have deliberately engaged in scatological and gutter language (think back to my use of words in Chapter One) – it is meant to be a jolt to your lethargy. The use of these words also creates an impression and moves you from one particular state to another. It did, didn't it? This move from state to state with the use of words is of particular relevance when speaking; if you're listening to this on Audible or as an audiobook, you most definitely will have been jolted by the language I used in Chapter One. Not least because I YELLED at you.

Language has the power to move us, the use of words also has the ability to destroy – consider the rhetoric (if you can call it that, it may be too polite a term) that Donald Trump engaged in that resulted in his election as U.S. President in 2016. "Lock her up," "Build the wall," "Send them back." Short, sharp, and to the point. It made his message super clear and easy to understand, sadly for the world and harmony among people. You get my point. Language is EVERYTHING. It is true to say that as humans we communicate only through our words in a limited way; about 7% of human communication is processed through words and language. Nevertheless, the conscious awareness of the words we are using is fundamental to our power in the world – our ability to dominate in the bedroom or the boardroom, as well as providing us with the wisdom to know when submitting is a more effective tactic in negotiating a scenario than being the boss.

Think about it in your case – what language are you using about yourself? Are you saying, "I can't do that," "that will never work," "that's not for me," "they're better than me," "I'll never get what I want?" Or are you saying to yourself, "let's get to it," "I'll have a go and see what happens," "I don't like this and that about the way you did that, perhaps you could try it like this?" The use of words creates a world, right? I know. Your words can create the impression that you are a doormat and can be walked all over, or they can create the impression that you're in charge and DO NOT MESS WITH YOU. They can imply that you are bored, apathetic, and essentially dry and dead, or they can leave people with a feeling of being inspired and called into action. Which do you use?

Can you see that the language you use when you talk about yourself, your life, your business, the people that matter the most to you, or even the world in general, is mostly negative, disempowering, and rooted in cynicism? It looks to all intents and purposes like it is a realistic perspective, but is actually just you gaslighting yourself and everyone around you. Forget what anyone else might be doing to you (or you are allowing them to do, let me be clearer about that). Are you using insipid, beige, and semi-comatose language to create the world in which you reside? Or is your language more like a David Hockney picture – full of vibrant color and sunshine? What's the purpose of my pointing out my use of language to you in the chapter about owning it? Well it's this: what language and words did you select to create your code of conduct and ethics? Are you satisfied with the vocabulary and literary tools that you have used to evoke the emotions and the feelings that you wish to experience when you are relating with your code of conduct and ethics?

Your code of conduct is designed and intended to call you forth into action and into the world in whatever way works best for you – think of it like Churchill's stirring "We will fight them on the beaches" speech, or Martin Luther King's "I have a dream." Your code of conduct may not be a particularly fine piece of oratory or rhetoric. That's fine, it's not for public consumption – it's for you. But it "should" and could stir you into action in a way that you have not been stirred before, and you "should" feel that stirring in areas of your body that, up to now, may have been entirely dormant. And by that, I'm going back to your pussy again.

Does your code of conduct and ethics make you feel wet and tingly? Yes? AMAZING!!! No…? OK, time to take another look at it then. You may be wondering at this point, that's all very well for you to say Suzanne, but what about yours? Good point. Yes… I have a code of conduct and ethics for myself, and yes, it really royally turns me on every time I engage with it. Trust me when I tell you that I am living inside of my code of conduct and ethics all the time I am writing this book, and it makes the process of the writing way easier, and a WHOLE lot more pleasurable – and since you asked… my code of conduct and ethics is this: I am the source of fun, freedom, and fulfillment in the world, for all people, such that war is consigned to history. Inspiring stuff, right? Yes, I think so. So, go have another look at your code of conduct and ethics and let's get your pussy juiced up again.

CHAPTER FOUR

YOU MUST BE CLEAR, COMMITTED AND CONSISTENT

Now you know the importance of paying attention to the language that you use and choose to create your universe, you can really start to see why I had you examine your beliefs and your motivations, as well as your goals right up front of this book. You burned the shit out of your old stories – literally sent them up in smoke. And you started carving your own version of David or painting your own Mona Lisa. You articulated your code of conduct and ethics, and you have become much more aware of how you use words and the world you create with your words. All that and you are only just starting Chapter Four –

Wow… did you expect that when you picked up this book? I doubt it.

All of this is great, and there's still so much more work to do… Now is the time to get focused (clear) and be committed and consistent. The best analogy I have for this is a story straight from nature. A few years ago, I was lucky enough to go on safari in the north of South Africa in one of their national parks. It was truly an extraordinary experience; I saw all of the big five that they have – elephant, rhinos, leopards, buffalo and lions. The whole thing was unforgettable, but a moment that stands out for me involves watching a lion stalking a hyena and then catching the prey and the ruthless efficiency of the hunt, kill and eating the meat. It was humbling, scary, sad, and supremely impressive. The focus, clarity, and ruthless efficiency were astonishing. In the blink of an eye, the lion had moved from 500 meters away to devouring the hyena and protecting the meat for the pride. It was a lesson in the power of focus. The lion had been completely focused on its prey, it was clear on its intention, and that intention was manifest faster than a speeding bullet. That's the power of being focused, clear, committed, and ruthlessly consistent.

Focus gets you what it is that you want. When you put focus on something, it is like heat under water, like I already said! Do you remember your chemistry lessons at school? You perhaps had a beaker full of water, and the teacher asked you to stick a Bunsen burner underneath it. What happens when you heat up the water? It starts to boil, and eventually, it transmutes into steam. That's what focus provides. If you shoot a laser at a glass, it starts to cut through the glass, the power of focus is how a martial artist is able to bust through a pile of concrete blocks. It's also how a yogi is able to stand on their head for a seemingly interminable amount of time.

Being very clear about those top 100 experiences you have articulated in Chapter One, and then super laser-focused on fulfilling them (notice how I took ownership of the word laser-focused there) in whatever order you choose to go for them, is what will have you actually experience those 100 experiences that you are seeking and craving for in your life. So if you want to create screaming orgasms in your bedroom, and what's in the way of that is the embarrassment you feel about how your body is, first of all, find some compassion for yourself. Then ask yourself, if having screaming orgasms is on your top 100 list, to apply some focus to it, look at what's causing the embarrassment about the state of your body – then work out what you want to do it about it, take action, put some focus in, and get stuck in.

Suzanne in 2005 ©Julia Pool 2005

Suzanne in 2006 ©Julia Pool 2006

Suzanne in 2012 ©Suzanne Pool 2012

Suzanne in 2015 © 2015 Suzanne Pool

Suzanne NOW! © 2020 Becky Rui

Just so you know, I practice what I preach here. I have applied my thinking to my own body. As you can see from the photographs that I have included here and throughout the book, I have lost and gained weight repeatedly during my entire adult life. But over the past three years from writing this book (June 2020), I have lost close to 100lbs, and I've done it through very dedicatedly and deliberately applying focus and energy to that area of my life. Don't get me wrong. I had bariatric surgery in September of 2017, and I say that very intentionally and without fear of being judged. Yes, I had surgery. I did it because once I hit 40, losing weight became harder and harder, I was eating less and less food, and exercising more and more intensively. With ZERO results.

I took a very drastic action, mostly because my heroic surgeon let me know that I was not crazy; it does get harder to lose weight when we hit middle age. He also helped me understand that it seemed that there was something not working in my metabolic system and that surgery would sort it out. Finally, he was the first doctor I had ever met that managed to leave me feeling like this was not a unique problem and that I was not super stupid for being fat. I am a Cambridge educated former lawyer. I know that I am far from being stupid, but I was very judged for being fat, and more importantly, I was really judging myself. I took a very deliberate, massive action in the area of my health and well-being. My surgeon took 70% of my stomach out of my body, permanently.

But here's the thing: I thought that would be the solution – it was drastic and interventionist. It wasn't. I have worked really bloody hard over the last three years to lose the weight. I have put hours in at the gym, I have tracked what I eat, day in and day out, I have learned to love running (I really hated running, now surprisingly I enjoy it, and I am for sure no gazelle – I am short and stocky as you can see in my photos!), I have cultivated a very dedicated yoga practice. You will learn much more about my feelings and experience with movement in a forthcoming chapter. Just to say here that I had to put virtually ALL my focus on this area, apply a lot of concentration, and commit massively to the actions that it was going to take. And you know what? I am really proud of myself. I have worked hard and diligently over a considerable amount of time, and it has paid off.

I have also been persistent. You may have noticed I said that I have lost weight many times over the years. That's true – I have lost near enough 90lbs about three times since I turned 30, and I'm only 46 as I write this book. My mother first took me to a Weight Watchers class when I was 14, so you know, I've really battled my weight since I was a child. And I don't know as I write this that I won't regain weight at some time in the future, I may. What I know is that I know what to do about it if I do, and I can intervene on myself quickly; I weigh myself every single day of my life, including when I'm on vacation (I travel with bodyweight scales!) and I measure myself at least once a month. I am committed, and I am consistent with these practices.

Sometimes, I have to deal with myself slightly about them – particularly when the scale number goes up instead of down, but that's part of the point. I have developed a set of habits that work for me; I have clarity about what works for me and what does not work for me nutritionally, with exercise, with drinking water, and with sleep. It's like a mixing desk, an analogy that I will give you much more fully later on. I have the levers, and I know how to manage them – I can dominate my body, and you can too. But I had to put the work in to make that happen. It has taken being clear about my goal and being utterly committed to the fulfillment of that goal, and finally, I have been very consistent with the habits and practices that it takes to make it happen.

Did you know that The Beatles were turned down by at least three major record labels before they were finally signed to Parlophone in 1961? Did you know that one A&R man (the role accountable in a record label) said of The Beatles they will never amount to anything? Um. Oh dear. Mistake. But that's not the point of the story, the point is this – Lennon and McCartney – they didn't give up. They got no, and they kept going until they met George Martin, and then they hit the big time. It's the same with Britney Spears. Britney Spears looks like an overnight success – she hit it with *Baby One More Time* when she was only 17 years old. It was her first single, and it was a global Number One. But what we don't see with her story is that she had been a Mouseketeer (on the Disney Channel) since she was 11 years old, she had been at dance school since she was seven years old and she had been practicing, practicing, practicing, basically since she could walk.

That is what it takes to dominate whatever you want in your life. If you want to dominate your business and right now, it feels like you are beholden to your shareholders or the bank, you have to find out what you are aiming for, and then practice and practice and practice shooting for that aim, again and again, and over again. If you want to dominate in the bedroom, then think about how that looks for you, share that vision with your partner, and execute it, get the whip out, and give him the lashing you desire. If you want to be served in a certain way, whether it is in the bedroom, boardroom, or the bar, hold the vision of it, and make it happen by practicing, practicing, and practicing again.

Take the time to learn what works for you, what turns you on, what lights your fire, what makes your pussy juicy. Dwell on that; it matters – not just to you, but to the world at large. That's why I asked you to create your list of top 100 experiences that you want in your life. Then get committed to fulfilling that list and get to work. Be persistent and persevere.

Perseverance and persistence pay – this is where the subtle discernment I mentioned in the chapter about language really comes into play. When you are committed, consistent, persistent, and you persevere, you find that the universe starts to conspire in your favor; the results that you are seeking start to manifest and you have MUCH better data to quantify and qualify the results with. The mixing desk starts to have a life of its own. You start to be able to discern which of your actions are giving you the biggest bang for your buck, so you can invest less and make more. It's extraordinary. And it takes work, so YOU MUST DO THE WORK.

CHAPTER FIVE

You Must Investigate and Do Some Detective Work

How about we take a little time now to look at how you discover what it is that is really important to you. I know you've created your top 100 list of experiences that you want in your life. How easy was that for you? Did that list just flow? I doubt it.

It doesn't usually because it takes something to uncover what really matters to you and what is important. As I said in the previous chapter, being persistent and persevering really make a difference.

It's a drag, I know. I really prefer an easy life too, but unfortunately, life isn't like that, and actually, that's where the juice of life truly is. If life were all reclining on beds eating grapes, like Dionysus in Roman times, we would all be as big as houses and falling over with Type 2 diabetes, oh… wait… we are. But not because life is easy, it's more that mostly because in the West in the late 20th and early 21st centuries we have become complacent and lazy. We have become more interested in being comfortable and safe. Unfortunately, this has led to many of us becoming flabby and unfit over the years, just as I was, I have already told you my story on that score.

Being comfortable is easy; it's safe, and in the moment of it happening, it feels better, but it is like a McDonald's meal. It sounds good in the moment, but you feel pretty crappy when you start digesting it, and about two hours after you ate the thing you wonder what on earth you were thinking about walking into the restaurant, let alone eating the food. Being comfortable and safe is like that. Do you have a pair of mom jeans or stretchy tracksuit (velour) bottoms that you wear on a "fat" day, and actually, you have found recently that you have been wearing those nasty jeans or tracksuit bottoms rather more often than you realized? That's the feeling of comfort that I am thinking of. It looks like it's safer and more comfortable, but it's like those gnarly insidious limiting beliefs and decisions that we looked at way back in Chapter Two. They eat away at your self-esteem. They cause your risk and courage muscles to atrophy. THEY'RE BAD FOR YOUR HEALTH! Stop wearing them. Stop eating the nasty food. Put the mom jeans and the tracksuit bottoms in the trash can (bin) where they deserve to be!

Here's the thing: life begins at the edge of your comfort zone. That was written by one Neale Donald Walsch in his seminal spiritual work *Conversations with God*. It's true. Being scared and uncomfortable leads to growth and development in your life. Yes, it can be painful, that's actually a good thing (and I will explain that more fully later on in the book), it is almost certainly uncomfortable, but it is also the juice of life. How come? Because it's exciting, it's challenging, it stretches you to strive for a place or an experience that you may not have attempted, let alone attained EVER before. And oh yes, what does that mean? IT'S FUCKING WELL FUN.

I know I'm not the only one that likes a roller coaster. They make me quake in my boots as I think about them, and when I'm in a line at an amusement park for a coaster, I frequently think WHAT ARE YOU DOING? But then I find myself at the front of the line, and with trepidation, I strap myself in. Five minutes later, having thrown myself upside down and round about a few times in my seat, at great velocity, I am walking away from the coaster as high as a kite. Because yes, I am thrilled that I had a go and expanded myself to take that risk.

As Eleanor Roosevelt, wife of FDR, the U.S. President during the Depression and the Second World War, is frequently quoted as saying, "*Do One Thing EVERY Day that Scares You.*" Life begins when you start to uncover what really matters to you, what gives you a thrill, what gives you chills, and what turns you on. So do the detective work and investigate what is important to you. Consider your top 100 experiences that you are seeking to accomplish – do you want to refine the list? Are there experiences that you want to add to it? Can you enhance those experiences? What can you begin with? As Johann Goethe said, *"Indecision brings its own decision. And days are lost lamenting over lost days. Are you in earnest? Seize this very minute. Whatever you do or dream you can do, BEGIN it. Genius has power and magic in it."*

Take a look at the resources you have available to you. Do what I have been taught to call an inventory of resources. What is available to you? What support do you have? Who is behind you? Who can you count on?

When you really engage in these questions, you will start to notice that actually, while you have family and friends that are very important to you, and it is critical that you recognize them and that, the reality is that YOU are the one you can count on most, you are the most support you have available to you, and you are your own greatest resource. This does not mean to say that you are the most important person in the world. I have already asked you to stop being self-centered and self-actional. You are not the most important person in the world. You are part of a much bigger picture, and you are just an aspect of that picture (a mere brushstroke if you will). BUT (and it is a big but) that does not give you permission to diminish yourself either. That is what I mean when I say you are your own greatest resource. Do you trust yourself? Do you really believe that anything is possible (we looked at that earlier in Chapters One and Two)? This is what I mean when I say that you are your own best friend and that you are your greatest resource.

You are going to take another minute now to assess the way you think and speak about yourself. I know, you feel like I keep asking you to do that. And you are right. I do. Repetition is the mother of skill. Practice, practice, practice – remember that? Go on then. Have you started journaling yet? You may not have done; I have not specifically asked you to do that. I'm asking you to do that now. Get yourself a decent sized journal (separate from the one that you are doing the exercises of this book in) – ideally letter sized if you are in the U.S. or A4 as we say everywhere else. Not one of those small little notepads. You are deserving of a proper full-sized journal. You have things to say, and you need a place to write them down! So from this point forward, I invite you to start journaling every day, ideally pretty much before you get out of bed in the morning.

If you have ever read *The Artist's Way* or heard of an author called Julia Cameron (who was married to the very well-known film director Martin Scorcese) you will be familiar with the process called *Morning Pages*. I'm not saying write three pages of your full-size journal (unless you want to). It's up to you how much you write in your journal. I am saying cultivate a new habit, daily, of writing in your journal. Journaling is a mysterious phenomenon. It seems like a really easy thing to do, and yet when you sit down (or lie down as I usually am when I'm writing my journal pages, and yes, I do this every day too) to write, it can seem incredibly daunting. I have known many days of journaling where all I have written for three pages is "I don't know what to write." I have quite seriously written nothing but that for an entire three pages of A4 in my journal. And yet there are some days where three pages are just not enough, and I have to stop myself over-indulging my writing habit. The point is this, I write. Daily. It gives me access to how I think and feel about myself and what is going on in the world and in my life. It was my original point of entry for writing this book.

When you journal, as I have already said, you start to notice, very acutely, how you talk about yourself, and others, and what you think about yourself and others. You may very well start to notice that the worst gaslighter you have in your life is not outside of you. It is, in fact, you. When you see that, transformation is possible. It is only through awareness and observation that you can start to see your own patterns – that's why you have to do some detective work and investigation. Get it? The antidote when you finally start to see how cruel you have been to yourself in the past is this:

Do the work and the exercises that I have given you already, and that I will continue to make available to you throughout the rest of this book. The work is hard though. Have you found yourself getting to this point and just merrily reading along? That's quite normal, but it will not make much difference. If that's you – and you are really interested in making some changes and starting to dominate your life and your business the way you have seen can be possible, then get in touch – NOW –

The grandfather of personal development and self-help – Jim Rohn – he mentored the big daddy of the industry, Tony Robbins, back in the 1970s and early 1980s, has frequently been quoted as saying we are the sum of the five people that we spend the most amount of time with. Curious that I would write that, just after I have been expounding the virtues of you being your own best friend, and having you start to notice that you can also be your own worst enemy. It is deliberate. Just like everything else that I have written and am writing. How come? Because now, you have started to realize the extent of your limited thinking. You can also start to see how the people that you are surrounded with are thinking in similarly limited ways.

I mentioned that being supported (perhaps by me) to undertake the journey that I am espousing in this book is a good idea. But when you take a long hard look at the people that you surround yourself with, are they capable of being your Sherpa on the journey – you know, like the Sherpas in the Himalayas who will carry you up the mountain if you need them to? No? OK, are the people you surround yourself with even capable of going on the journey with you? This is the actual question. How do you feel about engaging your five people in this intimate, challenging self-enquiry? Does it fill you with glee and eagerness? Or are you screaming and shouting at me, wanting to put the book down? I suspect it is the latter. If it is, fret ye not. It is common. What is uncommon is to find people that are willing to accompany you on this journey.

CHAPTER SIX

You Must Stop Tolerating Things (and People)

It takes MASSIVE courage and commitment. A willingness to own the tough stuff, in order to create the life that you truly want and to experience all that life has to offer. The sad truth of it is, though, that it is a rare individual that is willing to engage. So, pat yourself on the back for having gotten this far, and start the process of asking who you want to accompany you and who you want to be surrounded by. Earlier in Chapter Three, I mentioned people in your life that you realize are not good for your self-esteem, are not empowering, and might be actively disempowering.

I have had a fair few of them in my life. Not least my mother, whom I have already told you about. But also, the odd boyfriend here or there. I am pretty good at standing my ground and knowing what my boundaries are around people respecting me and being supportive, but occasionally one of them gets through the cracks. When they do, it can be soul-destroying (temporarily) until I come to my senses and kick them to the curb. So have a look at your list and check out who is around you most closely. Are they positive influences that support you and encourage you to pursue your dreams? Are you that way for them? Check – to both counts? Yes? Good, cherish these relationships and nurture them. No? What do you want to do about it? Keep them in your life? Talk to them about how they leave you feeling. Check in with yourself about how you may be leaving them feeling? Or kick them to the curb. The choice is yours. Work it out for yourself and take action.

By the way, it may make you happy to know that all this rigorous self-enquiry and examination of your life and the people in it has a benefit that you may not be aware of. Two thousand five hundred years ago, Socrates articulated that "*the unexamined life is not worth living.*" In 2020, Suzanne Pool is saying to you that not only is the unexamined life not worth living, she is saying that living an unexamined life could age you. Engaging your brain and your mind in the type of enquiry you are doing as you work your way through this book keeps your brain active, and ensures your neural pathways continue to be clear and engaged. This keeps you younger. You are preventing your brain from atrophying. So please stick with it.

While you are about keeping your mind engaged and your brain active, I am going to remind you of the importance of tracking and tracing. You may not realize this, but as I write this, the world has been in the midst of the 2020 COVID-19 outbreak. Track and trace has become synonymous with the attempt to control the virus and manage the impact of the outbreak. Whether that has been successful mostly depends on the country you are in. I am not commenting on the effectiveness of track and trace in relation to the containment of the virus. I am going to say that track and trace is useful in your life. I have already asked you to look at the people that you spend the most amount of time with. Make a call for yourself about whether they are life-enhancing people for you, and you for them. Or whether as you reflect on what you want in your life and how you are now choosing to live your life, these are people that are not life-affirming for you. Track and trace is not just about the people in your life though.

Track and trace is about looking at what you are measuring. Remember I asked you to measure things? Maybe not, I have only really casually mentioned it up to now. But let me just say this about track and trace. What you measure, moves. If you want more money in your bank account, but you never look at your bank balance, how are you going to know whether you are accomplishing your aim of bringing more money into your life or not? It seems obvious, really. But you would be surprised. What do you measure in your life? What are you tracking for your success? Are you, in fact, tracking anything?

You already know my weight loss journey, particularly over the last three years, as I write this book. What I have realized as I have gone through my life is that this track and trace, metric and measure is not only in relation to weight. It really applies to everything; if you want to become wealthier and a more effective manager and gatherer of money, then track your spending, track your income, have a plan to keep your spending within boundaries and track your net worth – whether it goes up or down. Just like the number on the scales which sometimes goes up when you have put in massive effort to make it go down, net worth does that too. We have to cultivate a way of being about the number, that it is just that – A NUMBER. It does not mean anything about us. It is not personal to us. It is not physically attached to us as a label for all to see. It is just a number. When it goes up, it goes up (net worth YAY! weight on the scales – BOO!). When it goes down, it goes down (converse relationships for net worth and weight). It does not make us more successful or a "better person." The number just is. Let it be but know what it is.

I know this chapter is a long one. It's also a deep one; we have talked about a lot of uncomfortable subjects during this time together. It's the tough stuff that makes you stronger, so please… stick with me, baby. I casually mentioned earlier that doing this rigorous self-enquiry actually keeps you younger. I didn't tell you it helps you stave off Alzheimer's (keeping your brain engaged and active prevents that atrophy at the heart of the proven causes of Alzheimer's). It also helps keep you healthy as you advance in age – keeping your mind active helps with heart and blood health too. Although to be fair, the next chapter is much more relevant to you in the prevention of the onset of aging physically (the next chapter is the one all about exercise and movement, in case you are wondering). My point is this, doing this work, uncomfortable and challenging though it may be, is virtuous and rewarding, so acknowledge yourself for your commitment to living your best life and building your best business.

On that positive note, I am going to take us down another dark tunnel, just briefly, before we move on to more positive matters in the next chapter – yes, you are getting toward the end of this challenging, confronting part of the journey. Before we get there though, I want to ask you one last stomach-churning question. And actually, it is probably the most important question of any of the enquiries I have asked you to engage in throughout this chapter: What are you tolerating?

Toleration is insidious. Many of us have been brought up to think that toleration is a liberal value to be respected and honored. I say it is not. I recall a conversation with my mother when I was a teenager about the toleration of the Jewish community in the U.K. I identify as Jewish, although my father was Christian and from the U.K., and my mother was Jewish and American. Inter-faith and international marriage in the mid-20th century was somewhat more unusual than it is in the early 21st century. My parents had to be very deliberate in where they lived in London to ensure that my brother and I would not feel "different" at school. Our schools were carefully curated for that purpose, and we were socialized in communities that had families similar to ours – not an easy feat, even in liberal, diverse London in the 1980s. And yet, as diverse as our communities were, I still felt different. I felt "tolerated." I was neither Jewish nor Christian. I was neither British nor American. I was "other," but I was sort of OK, so I could stay. It was an uncomfortable experience of never quite belonging.

Now, I'm not going to tell you that you have to belong. For sure not, this book is about standing out, and dominating your spaces – the discipline it takes to be willing to stand out in all areas of your life. But I am going to tell you that toleration is insidious. You are not embracing and fully accepting what is in your life. Neither are you willing to do what it takes to have whatever it is, change and transform into a situation that is to your desire and wanting. That is just not OK. It's apathetic. It's dull. And if you were someone that was willing to live that way, you would not have read this far into this book. You probably wouldn't even have picked up this book. So, I know, that's not you.

You are interested in being the boss of you, and all in your domain. So then, I ask again – what are you tolerating? Are you willing to do the detective work to find out what you are tolerating?

Is it the clutter in your home? Is it the spices in the cupboard in your kitchen that are long past their use-by date? Is it the relationships with people that you think are your friends, but when you actually look – um, yeah... Nah. Is it the gaslighting way that you speak to yourself and the negativity of your thinking?

Make a list… down one side of a page in your journal, the one that you are doing the book exercises in.

Do the work. Take the time. I know it's not comfortable. I've made sure of that. Toleration is icky. It's patronizing and vaguely sneering. "*I don't like this being the way that it is, but I really can't be bothered to do anything about it.*" It's passive-aggressive. And you're not passive-aggressive. I don't tolerate passive-aggressive people around me. You would not be reading this book if you were passive-aggressive. So, go on… have a real look. Pick up the rug that you have been avoiding and look at the pile of dust underneath it. Smelly? Good! The smellier, the better. You are going to be able to clean that shit up, and then some!

Have you done your list? Yes? Good. Now have a look at it. You have only written on one side of the page, yes? OK. Here's what to do with the other side of the page. What are you going to do about each of those things that you are tolerating? Each of those relationships, that insidious way that you talk and think about yourself, the gaslighting "friend" you thought you had. Put as many actions as you can see to do on the list. Now choose the first one.

AND GO TAKE THAT ACTION. In each case. Take the action. I appreciate this is uncomfortable. I am asking you to do something that you have never done before. I get that. But this is about you dominating your life, your intimate life, and your business. So, trust me, it is worth it.

Now that you have taken those actions, get in touch with me (all-eyes.suzannepool.com), show me the list, with the actions, and the outcomes so far. I'm really, truly wanting to know. I am proud of you for taking this action and doing what it takes. It's tough, and it shows that you have what it takes. Once you have sent that email, please celebrate and acknowledge yourself. It's a courageous, willing woman that is ready to engage in this exercise. I commend you.

CHAPTER SEVEN

You Must Embody the Process

It's a bit of a word of the zeitgeist that "embody" thing. Have you read about it in *Cosmo* or *Psychologies*? I know I have. It's hard to know what it means though. Embody? Huh? I get that. In a nutshell, we feel and experience things and life in our whole bodies. Most of us walk around the world living in our heads. You're always focused on how you think, what to say, how to respond. All of which is useful, but generally speaking only involves about 10% of your capacity for experiencing the world. Science is starting to identify and research the connection between our ability to make decisions and take action in the world – and our bodies from the neck down. This is what I mean about embodying the process.

You remember that all the way through the book I have been, quite briefly but actually quite critically, banging on about the importance of practicing yoga? Here's where that rubber meets the road. We are going to look, in depth, in this chapter at the importance of moving your body, and in particular, in practicing yoga – which I would say is my personal preference for the most complete form of exercise that I know. Exercise is really critical in the process of creating you as being the best that you can be, getting your sexy back and having you dominate in the bedroom, boardroom and beyond as you desire.

It's probably a trite thing to say – we all know the age-old formula for losing weight and feeling our best. It is eating less and moving more. True. But exercise is sooooooo much more than that! And that's why I am devoting an entire chapter to it, very early on in the book. I am truly an evangelist for the importance of movement. And I choose to call it movement, rather than exercise per se. The difference is important actually; movement is about that thing I spoke about last chapter – flexibility and adaptability. The use of the word is also critical – I will say more about the importance of language in a future chapter. So, let's make an agreement between us for now – we're calling it movement.

Now that is established, how about we look at the difference that movement makes, and why it is so critical for embodying this process. Adding movement to your daily life is the first consistent habit I am going to TELL, I'm not asking, I'm literally telling you, to implement – with discipline. Ideally, it should be one of the first things that you do with your day (after you have done your journaling). Get out of bed and MOVE! It doesn't have to be much – a 20-minute walk around the block that gets your heart pumping slightly is really all I DEMAND that you do. But I do demand that you begin it. I also demand that you keep it going. If you stop, start again. Don't beat yourself up, don't dwell on any of those gnarly thoughts we talked about in an earlier chapter; just get out and walk.

Why should I, you might be asking yourself… Good question. Here's why – movement alters your mood. It's a total state changer. Your perception of yourself will change. Your ability to think differently comes fully into being. You might lose weight – I'm not going to promise that, because losing weight is 80% nutrition, unfortunately. I wish it weren't that way. I LOVE food, and I love to eat whatever the hell I like. Sadly, I have learned over many years, that just does not work, and no amount of slogging it out on a treadmill is going to make the difference. But I'm not asking you to slog it out on a treadmill. I'm demanding that you go out and get some fresh air and hopefully some vitamin D. While you are about it, why not have a go at some forms of movement that you may not have experienced before? I love that about exercise and movement. The diversity of forms of movement available to us is really amazing, and actually, this is where yoga really fits into the equation. Movement can take the form of walking, as I've indicated, running if you wish, cycling, swimming, dancing, Pilates, yoga, weight training, sword fighting, martial arts, tango, Zumba, or even Gyrotonic or Gyrokinesis – have you heard of them? If you haven't,

Google them. I personally like weight training, a variety of forms of cardio exercise, and Ashtanga Yoga.

Movement has you learn about yourself; generally speaking, any form of movement that you engage in requires presence of mind. More about presence of mind later, but for now, let's just say this – if you practice weight training, as I do – here are some photos of me lifting silly weights! – you will know that when lifting a heavy weight (or really just any weight at all) if you are not present and focused when you do that, you are highly likely to drop it, and in the process do yourself an injury, or worse still break a toe or something (I've definitely had a few bruises from not being present when I was lifting, and I've broken a mirror or two…). The presence of mind required to undertake weight training is not why I do it though.

Suzanne Weight Training at Salecca (her gym)
© 2019 SALECCA LIMITED

Suzanne lifting a heavy bar at Salecca
© 2019 SALECCA LIMITED

Most women have an image of weight training that includes large, brawny (frequently not very brainy) men wearing wife-beater t-shirts with large, tight, wide belts on, grunting as they bench press a lot of weight on a bar that is too heavy for them. It's a fair assessment but does not do justice to the miracle that weight training actually is. Weight training requires massive discipline (there's my favorite word again) and commitment. It's not for the faint of heart – it hurts, often A LOT (and not because I've broken or bruised my toes). But it is TREMENDOUSLY empowering. I love that I know that I am as strong as any man. I do not need help with my bags when I get off a plane – I can pick them up with one hand (even the bags that weigh over 30kg {approaching 70lbs}). Yes, it is the case – women can be as strong as many men. Like I said, it takes discipline and commitment, but it is possible. Oh, and if you're sitting there thinking that's all great, but it's going to make me muscly and look like those men in tight vests – NO! Women can become more muscular with training, but we are NEVER going to be bulky. How come? Simply put, we do not have the cojones for it. Huh? Yes, you did read that correctly – we, as women, do not have the bollocks to become bulky; it comes down to hormones and, in particular, testosterone. We simply do not have enough. And a good thing too. I like being a woman.

Weight training is also very grounding. You have to root yourself right into the floor to be able to deadlift over 220lbs {100kgs}. Being that stable on one's feet is useful. It creates a surety and security that means anything is possible – remember anything is possible thinking from

Chapter One? When we have a strong foundation in our feet that goes up through our legs (the largest muscles in your body are in your legs and your bum), it translates to a certainty in our being that supports us in giving up those shitty little gnarly beliefs you identified in the earlier chapters. So, you know, that's what I really mean when I say you've got to embody the process. You are strong, you are capable – you are the boss of you – in the bedroom, the boardroom and beyond. Weight training is one of your keys to success. Trust me, find a personal trainer at a good gym and give it a go – for at least six months, that's how long it takes for women actually to see the results of weight training start to show up. If you can't find a decent personal trainer, get in touch with me. I can help you. Weight training is almost the embodiment of discipline for me... not quite, but almost.

So, if weight training isn't the embodiment of discipline for me, then what is? Good question. Simple answer. Ashtanga Yoga.

I love yoga. I love yoga so much for the impact it has, not just on my body, but on the whole of my life and being, that I am a teacher. In yoga, it could be a gentle Hatha class, a flowing vinyasa style class, a super dynamic Ashtanga practice (like mine), or a really lovely stretchy yin or restorative yoga practice. It doesn't matter – it's the movement that matters. Yoga, to me, is like water. It's fluid and flexible, it flows, and I do mean yoga flows, not you. You will definitely flow in yoga. But yoga means "unity." Yoga is about creating a sense of well-being in the world. The goal (if there is one) of practicing yoga is accomplishing the state of samadhi or universal bliss and peace. That's the experience of flow. If you're interested to learn more about experiencing flow, I highly recommend a book, helpfully called *Flow*, by Mihaly Csikszentmihalyi. It goes into a lot of detail about the state of flow that one experiences when you're connected to the universe, and you are totally "in" the action. This state of flow – when you're present to being present, and all that gnarly stuff in your head quiets down – is actually the point of movement, and the point of yoga in my book. Yoga is the most effective way that I know (and I've spent a lot of time and a lot of money seeking this space) of finding your flow and generating being present in your life.

Yoga promotes flexibility and adaptability, not just in your body (it definitely does that too) but in your mind, and your spirit as well. It's probably pretty obvious how yoga promotes flexibility in body – I articulated the experience of flow in the previous paragraph. What does that mean for your mind in particular? You remember that story you set fire to in Chapter One – you did set fire to it, didn't you? Is there anything you have noticed about the way that you think since you set fire to your story? My intention with that action was to provide a space for something new to open up for you. Something new, something unexpected, and to provide a space for you to create new thoughts. That's what yoga does for your mind.

Yoga is not just a physical experience, it's very much a mental one too; there is the whole philosophy element that accompanies yoga, and I'm really into that as well, but that's not the purpose of this book (well it is, but only indirectly). Yoga is a mental experience – stretching your body into forms that you did not know you could accomplish, and perhaps discovering that you actually cannot do the poses, could be useful for your ability to think outside the box. Thinking outside the box was a buzz phrase of the late 20th century and the early 21st century. I was never quite sure what it meant. But for me, I think it is most effectively articulated as the ability to think new thoughts for you. The ability to look at a situation differently from your ordinary generalized perspective. The willingness to give up a long-held opinion in favor of finding an agreement – useful in a negotiation by the way that one. When you practice yoga, you have to give up being rigid, both in body – you'll fall over – and in mind. Some of the poses look like contortions; you have to engage your brain to consider how you might accomplish them. That's why I'm a total evangelist for yoga.

If you're interested in learning yoga with me or discovering the truly life-enhancing experience of lifting heavy weights (contradictions anyone?), then check out my website www. Suzannepool.com or drop me a message at all-eyes. suzannepool.com and we can explore that idea together. I 100% guarantee that is a decision you will NEVER regret.

One final thought (possibly a long one) about the benefits of movement in your life: emotions are actually energy and movement trapped in our bodies. E(nergy) and (e) motion (get it?). What does this mean for you? What it means is essentially – as I've been pointing at all through this chapter – movement causes transformation. The latest neuroscience research indicates that emotions do not live in our brains; in fact, they reside more accurately in our digestive systems (I will explain that in much more detail in the chapter about listening to your stomach). Research demonstrates now that the holding on to fat and other toxic experiences in our bodies is most often associated with the toxic retention of poisonous emotions – that's a core reason I had you burn your story so early on in the process of going through this book. It's also why you did such a detailed inventory of your gnarly limiting decisions and beliefs early on too. So, get out there and move that shit around! Shake it up… Roll down a hill like a kid. Find a field and scream at the top of your lungs and spin like a whirling dervish, beat the crap out of an old pillow that you really should throw away. All of these are AMAZING forms of movement for your body; they are also life-transforming moves for your emotions.

Hopefully, you are now really convinced of the benefits of daily movement, and yes, I do mean DAILY. Get to it!

CHAPTER EIGHT

You Must be Flexible and Adaptable

I love yoga. That is probably not a big surprise to you. I evangelized on that in the last chapter. I have also already told you throughout the earlier part of the book that I believe it is important to be flexible and adaptable.

I have not told you why I believe it is important to be flexible and adaptable in a book about discipline. I have not told you that practicing yoga is going to give you access to dominating your life, your body, your sex life, your business, and everywhere else you want to be in charge. The long and the short of it is this: being rigid and controlled is actually the counter to what it is to dominate your life. Surprised? I was too. But life is a dance, and when we are rigid in dance, it's just painful to watch, and frequently painful to participate in too... Think about all those dads that you have watched at weddings. Or remember Baby's sister in *Dirty Dancing*? You know the one, she was all control and toeing the line, but she was a rubbish, rubbish dancer (I can't even remember her name!). Patrick Swayze was never going to tell her father to get her out of the corner – the corner was where she actually belonged. That's my point, to be effective in life, we actually need to be able to move with agility and nimble feet; otherwise, we become like Godzilla, stomping our way through life.

So, I say it again, I love yoga. Yoga is many things, there is a whole philosophy of yoga that is truly fascinating, and I have to confess, I have stolen quite a lot of material (not directly, obviously) and themes from the philosophical texts of yoga, for this book. The rigorous self-enquiry is taken directly from the *Yoga Sutras of Patanjali*. The journey of the hero creating the life that is based on action, and not merely thinking about it, is taken directly from *The Bhagavad Gita* (and coincidentally inspired George Lucas in creating *Star Wars*). But don't let that I am throwing esoteric books and ancient texts at you get in the way of the point. Yoga is life. The asana of yoga creates flexibility and adaptability in your body that I GUARANTEE, if done consistently over time, translates directly into your life. If you really want to study yoga, then feel free to explore the philosophy and history which is fascinating and does give great insight into modern living. That isn't my point in this chapter though.

Stopping the Godzilla tail is my point. I am seeking to prevent you destroying everything in your life that is good and is working for the sake of you dominating everything around you. The discernment of knowing when action is required and when it is not is a VITAL ingredient in the recipe of you owning your life and taking control of all that you purvey.

You may be thinking that this message of flexibility and adaptability is contradictory to everything that I have already been saying throughout the book. I have implored you to undertake a rigorous examination of yourself. I have implored you to cast out the backstabbers around you masquerading as so-called "friends." I have implored you to write your story and then burn that bastard to ashes. And now I'm telling you, actually, what you already have maybe isn't that bad. Whiskey Tango Foxtrot, as they say on U.S. TV. What the actual fuck? Fair enough. And the answer to that is yes… and no. Of course it is! I'm encouraging you to be flexible and adaptable – geddit? LMAO. The enquiry that I have urged you to undertake is very important. The rigorous self-examination of life is where the real juice is. All I am now saying is, "Don't throw out the baby with the bathwater." Some of what you already have is useful and maintainable and well done for having it in your life. Keep going!

Some of your relationships, while not perfect, are pretty damn good. And as we all know, relationships are work. You don't just wake up one morning and find out you have been married to your husband for 50 years. It doesn't happen. Somewhere along the line of that 50 years, you (and he) put in some effort and energy in making that relationship functional. (I hope, at any rate, I suppose it is possible to sleepwalk your way through life for 50 years, I just can't imagine being able to do that!) In your inventory of relationships that I asked you to do a few chapters back, in Chapter Three, I believe, there were relationships that you rated highly, and that were functioning well for you. Good job! There are a couple of things that you can do with that information now that we are in the chapter about being flexible and adaptable.

1. You can acknowledge yourself for being a fully functioning adult – alive and well in the world! Yay!

2. You can assess them for what is working consistently over time. Do that – it will help you identify what does not work for you in the relationships you articulated as sub-optimal.

3. You can assess those relationships for common characteristics between them that can enable you to understand more of what works for you and what doesn't beyond the individual.

All of this deliberate action is useful and fundamental to the living of the good life, as we are creating here. No one has ever asked you to do work like this before, have they? Even after all those years of therapy, and spending thousands (if not tens of thousands of pounds, dollars or whatever your flavor of currency is), you have never really investigated for yourself what are the common characteristics of the relationships that work for you. I understand. It is not ordinary this work you are doing. That's why most people don't own their lives and dominate the spaces they operate in (positively dominate, I mean). Have I made you feel special and like you stand out yet? Yes? Good. Carry on!

So now you have taken that rigorous inventory of relationships that I have suggested, you have looked and you have found that there are relationships that work well for you. And others that… well… don't. What to do now? The first thing to do is this: acknowledge where you are. It is OK not to be OK. We cannot always be smiley, happy people all the time. In fact, it would be weird if you were – I would ask you what kind of drugs you were on. Life is simply not roses all the time. We all have versions of the gnarly, limiting beliefs that you uncovered in Chapter Two. Welcome to being human and acknowledging your humanity.

In addition, it is OK to notice that you have emotions that you find less than empowering some of the time. Maybe you have some anger that you are holding on to. Perhaps you feel afraid at times. I do. Trust me as I write this book, my gnarly thoughts start entering my head – what will people think of this? Am I getting too big for my boots that I am writing this? What if no one reads, or worse – wants to read the book? Then I start to feel afraid, and the words, they stop flowing as easily. Back to you – perhaps you feel some resentments or apathy. OK. You are a human being like the rest of us.

Some of your relationships are not working as optimally

as you would like them to. Got it. What now? The first step is to do exactly as you have just done. Acknowledge what is not working and make a pledge to do something about it. On the point about the pledge about doing something about it, please do not fall into the obvious pitfall in this scenario. You are not allowed to expect that doing something about this is going to involve anyone other than you. People do not change because you ask (or worse, expect) them to change. Relationships morph and transform because YOU changed; you did something about it. Remember, in Chapter One, I mentioned that the only thing preventing you from accomplishing what you want in the world and having the life that you desire was you. That applies here too. You are the one that is going to make the difference. You are the one that is doing the work. No one else.

That said, now there is some work to do on altering these relationships that you have declared as sub-optimal in your life. Start by conducting the same assessment that you did on your relationships that are working exactly as you want them to. That is:

1. Assess what is not working about the relationship.

2. Enquire into how that not working relationship leaves you feeling.

3. Examine whether you want to retain this relationship in your life (I imagine that since you are engaging in this enquiry that you do, otherwise you would not bother).

4. What is an expression of this relationship working perfectly for you?

Do this for each of the relationships that you have identified as being sub-optimal. Great. Now… it's time to grab your big girl knickers as we say in the U.K. And by that, I mean it is time to find your courage. And decide what action you want to take in relation to this relationship.

In most cases, this looks like having a conversation with the person with whom you are engaged in the relationship, and which you have identified the relationship as not working as optimally as you would like. Whoa… you mean I actually have to let someone know how I feel and that when I interact with them, I am left feeling less than ideal? Um… well… yes. You want to dominate your life – everywhere… in the bedroom, in the boardroom… everywhere? Yes, you are going to have to grow a pair of balls, (what is the female equivalent of generating that level of courage? Honestly, I have not found the phrase) and be vulnerable with that person.

I hated the word vulnerable; for me, it conjured up pictures of weakness and under attack. That is until I realized that being vulnerable is actually the most courageous act available to us as people. It was only in the act of being vulnerable – and admitting to another that you care about the relationship enough to acknowledge that this relationship leaves you less than empowered when engaging in it – that courage is manifest and you start to dominate (in reality) your life truly. Being vulnerable is really a demonstration of the greatest level of authenticity.

It is truly you being you. You are acknowledging to another that you love them and that the relationship between you really matters. This willingness is powerful, especially when you know that you are in control of your response to their reactions. You have the power to manage yourself and deal with whatever appears in front of you, or better yet, empower the relationship to move in the direction you want it to.

This willingness to be vulnerable is the key to dominating your life. It is also why it is vital that you learn to be flexible and adaptable. In sharing your discomfort in a relationship, alongside the sharing of the love that you feel inside the relationship, you create a space where transformation of that relationship becomes possible. I know. It has happened to me. For the past three and a half years as I write this book, I have been living with my brother in an apartment that I own. Our agreement when he came to share my apartment after we sold the family home in which he had been living, following our father's death, was that he was to move out after six months and that he would spend the majority of those six months staying with me, traveling. As it turned out, he did not actually travel until after the six months had passed, and he is still living in my apartment (three years later...!).

If you had asked any of my friends or family, some of whom have known us our entire lives, whether Ralph and I could live together for six months, let alone for three years, they would have laughed in your face. Ralph and I had a history of bickering with each other over the really little things; once he had even tried to get out of a car that I was driving while it was moving because we had had an argument. And yet, we have been quite happily living together for three years now. This is in itself a transformation, and is acknowledged as such by our community.

What is at the source of this transformation? – it's exactly what I am asking of you. A willingness to share our feelings with each other, inside a context that we love each other – he's my next of kin, and that we are our last remaining close family, so our relationship matters to both of us. In addition, we have learned to listen to each other without judgment, argument, or taking things personally. We have learned to listen to each other carefully and clearly, without any need to become defensive or aggressive with each other. Do we occasionally argue? You bet your ass we do, but we are able to apologize and create a listening space for each other quickly. That is the source of transformation, and it is a direct result of our ability to be flexible and adaptable with each other. We have opinions and perspectives, but we can suspend them for the sake of harmony and co-operation. We are not fixed in stone; we can be flexible and adaptable. This is true domination in action.

In those relationships that are not working, or not working in your most optimal way, what can you now see about how YOU are being in those relationships? Are you sticking to your point of view? Are you being the rock in the river that dams the flow? Are you being the judgmental and opinionated one? It can be difficult and challenging to acknowledge – after all, it is not necessarily very pretty. It is, however, the source of power for you, and the access to being able to dominate your life in the way that you want to. I will say more about this shortly, but for now, let me be very clear, giving up your point of view and being flexible with your opinions is powerful and to be explored carefully.

Stubbornness is more like a donkey – remember Eeyore? The character from *Winnie The Pooh*. Now admittedly, Eeyore is memorable, mostly for his impressive ability to be depressed and a nay-sayer. But really, how far away from being a nay-sayer is stubbornness as a pattern of behavior anyway? You feel me? And that's what I mean. It isn't! Holding on to your opinions for dear life may seem like an admirable quality. We are taught that sticking to our views is a virtue. But how conducive is it to effective relationships? The answer to that is simple: it is not. So, let's have a look at those relationships you have listed, and check in with the opinions and points of view that you are holding on to that may not be appropriate or useful in the maintenance of those relationships. Where can you see that the best course of action for you would be to let go of those opinions for the sake of harmony and well-being? Good, now go have those conversations from love and affinity!

Just to be clear though, I am not asking you to subjugate yourself to the relationship. People can often read what I have just suggested as martyrdom or the path to victimhood. It is neither of these. I am encouraging you to explore being submissive and creating flexibility in places and relationships that it has felt counter-intuitive to do so in the past. That does NOT mean that you are going to be a doormat. NO, NO, NO, NO, NO. There is a very clear line between subjugation and submission.

At this point, I feel that it is useful to explain what I mean in this context. And really, this is very much at the heart of my message to you. Subjugation is about seceding control to another. Submission is about service. It is also the place of power. Are you aware that in dominant/submissive relationships, the power in the relationship resides with the submissive? The commonly held perspective is that the power resides in the dominant. They are, after all, "dominant." It is a misconception. Who has the ability to call shots? To call time on the activity when play gets to the point that they are no longer willing to participate? The dominant? No. The submissive, that is who. In a respectful dom/sub relationship, the sub calls the shots, the dom determines the activity and the play. The dom is also there to push the boundaries, and to test the boundaries. But the moment the sub says no (which usually looks like a safe word), then play stops, and all bets are off. The submissive in the relationship is in service of the dominant and in service of the needs that the dominant identifies, but the submissive has the power.

Please remember that. It is critical in the whole message of the book. It is also the key point in the message about being flexible and adaptable in relationships. When you start to come from a place of being of service and actually listen to the people that matter to you, life will alter. I promise you. Listening, though, is a massively underrated skill. People think they listen, but trust me, the ability to listen and hear what is being said is almost as rare as diamonds. Listening is rare, mostly due to those gnarly limiting decisions and beliefs that we looked at earlier in Chapter Two. We have little voices in our heads, criticizing us, criticizing other people, judging our actions, judging the actions of others, and generally being a royal pain in the ass. These little voices interfere in our ability to do many things, but most importantly, they interfere with our ability to listen to people cleanly.

How often have you been in a conversation with someone – you have said something or asked a question, and the response has been completely off base with respect to the response you had been expecting? That's what I am talking about. People hear what they want to hear, not what is actually being said. They listen through the filters of their thoughts, feelings, and voices in their heads. By the way, when I say people, I mean you. It is time now for you to suspend your filters and actually start to listen to people. When you do, that is when the miracles happen. Not only do you start to listen to people and relate with them differently. That behavior is reciprocated and returned. Life is just better, and boom, you start to get more of what you want in life. Try it, I promise you, you will not regret it.

As I write this, the U.K., where I live, is just starting to emerge from the lockdown associated with the COVID-19 outbreak of the first half of 2020. The world is also reeling from the death of George Floyd at the hands (or knee, actually) of a Minneapolis police officer. Essentially, we are in a state of turmoil, that is, as the media likes to remind us almost without end, unprecedented. There is a lesson for us in this, which again demonstrates how important it is to be flexible and adaptable in life. Nothing in life is certain. We like to think that once we hit adulthood, life is stable and unchanging. Find your life partner, get married, find a home, have a family, go to work, come home, go to sleep, rinse and repeat, get your children through school and then maybe university, and become proud grandparents. It's the classic American dream, and U.K. middle-class tale. Except, as we live through the early part of the 21st century, events in the economy − the Global Financial Crisis of 2008, Brexit in the U.K., the COVID-19 pandemic − have demonstrated that the objects we viewed as sacred cows − jobs, homes, health, and economic well-being − are far from being the certainties we had become accustomed to them being.

When you really look at it, and you are starting to look, I know − you've come this far in the book, you must be! − you will see that actually nothing in life is set, we can be made redundant almost at will, divorce is really quite straightforward and easy to accomplish, we can pass our children on to someone else. All of life is a choice that we make for ourselves. When you boil it down to the basics, you are free, and you can choose. And when you realize that you are free, and you have choice, then you realize that nothing is set in stone. I resisted this for years and years. I wanted certainty and stability. It was only when I accepted that my life was more impactful and of service when I accepted life's uncertainty in general.

In the uncertainty of life, you start to release yourself from the bonds of good/bad and right/wrong. Releasing yourself from these arbitrary, externally imposed notions is the key to freedom for you – and by the way, it is also the access for you to dominate your life, everywhere. As you give up other people's notions of what you should or should not be, do or have, then you start to see that you have the choice to create whatever it is that you want. I can hear you arguing with me about this. I understand that, but please know that while I have compassion for the uncertainty and discomfort that this might present for you, I truly believe this is what you are looking for. It takes discipline to accept that you are free, no matter what your circumstances are. It takes discipline to accept that you have the freedom to interpret all that has gone before in your life. It takes discipline to accept that you have the freedom to create whatever it is that you want in your life. Are you willing to do the work? And to find the discipline that it takes to dominate your life? I believe you are… You've come this far. Why stop now!

CHAPTER NINE

Pain is Expansive and a Sign of Growth

Identifying that you have freedom is uncomfortable. Practicing yoga is uncomfortable. Becoming stronger in life is uncomfortable. All of these are life-affirming experiences and are signs of growth in us as people. And all of them hurt! I get it. Pain is something we prefer to avoid. The U.S. has had an epidemic of opioid abuse in the 21st century because of the over-prescription of pain medication by doctors in the 1990s and early 2000s. Pain, it's bad. Run away from it. That has been the mantra of life for most of the post-Second World War generations. I am telling you, think again. Pain is useful and an opportunity for growth. Engage with pain and embrace it as your friend.

This is controversial; I know that only too well. I appreciate you may, at this point, decide this book is no longer for you. I am ordering you to think again. You have come this far. You are a woman of strength, determination, commitment, and courage. Pain is something for you to embrace. Pain is something for you to learn from. Pain is something for you to explore and perhaps even enjoy. If you have children, then you will most likely know that the pain of labor becomes a distant memory the moment you hold your newborn baby in your arms. This is what I am talking about – we as women are willing to go through the pain of pregnancy, let alone labor, for the sake of bringing a new human into the world. That is to be admired, respected, and embraced in my view. Instead, we are given epidurals and the pain is numbed.

Now let's be clear, I'm no Jane Fonda acolyte either. I am not necessarily of the view "no pain, no gain." But I am going to say this: sometimes you want a good hard fuck, and it hurts. Sometimes, in yoga class, you are going to stretch yourself further than you have stretched your body before, and it hurts. In the gym, you might try lifting a weight that is heavier than you have lifted before, or for more reps than you have managed in the past. Trust me, this really bloody hurts! Pain is good and useful. It represents growth.

You're still not convinced. I get that. It seems totally counter-intuitive. Our Western culture is set up for comfort and ease. We are told to meditate for peace and ease. We are fed mindless TV dramas and soaps to ease our pain of having to work during the day. We are coddled as children when we fall over and scrape our knee.

It is also fair enough to say that sometimes pain is not good. Sometimes that pain is telling you something and you do need to pay attention. There is a difference between growth pain – which is useful – and injurious pain, when something really hurts because you have done some damage. If you lift a weight and your back starts to hurt (sharply) – PAY ATTENTION. That is your body telling you something. If you are in a relationship and your stomach and heart start feeling uncomfortable, PAY ATTENTION; they are telling you something about the relationship. I'm going to say more about this surprising correlation later. There is definitely pain that we do want to pay attention to. It is usually of a sharp quality and is designed to bring our attention to the painful part of us urgently.

The pain that I am suggesting is beneficial (and good), is actually down to growth, and is a more dull, stretchy, expansive pain. I reckon you have spent a lot of your life avoiding this type of pain too. Now it is time to step up and feel the pain and experience the growth in your life that you have been craving. Throughout the book I have been urging discipline as access to the dominance of your life, loves, and all that you want in your world. In the previous chapter, I went into the difference between subjugation and submission. I also explained that submission is actually access to dominance in the world. The real access to this dominance is a willingness to experience the pain, in submission, that you have been unwilling to feel up to now.

I like bondage. I like being tied up. I like being whipped. I also like tying my partner up and lashing them too. It challenges us. It creates trust in the relationship – we really have to articulate and communicate clearly with each other to manage the space of the play effectively. I also like the pain. It heightens my pleasure. Have you read *Fifty Shades of Grey*? It goes way further than E.L. James wrote of, but just to say kudos to her in starting to bring a conversation into the mainstream that, up to then, had really been stuck in the closet. The pain of a lashing or a strike can actually be playful and raise your awareness of touch and sensuality. Just to remind you, the submissive in a play relationship has the power. The submissive has the ability to control the limit and the line. In a respectful play relationship, pain is access to a heightened orgasm. Now I've got your attention, let's talk about the other ways that pain is useful to you.

You may have already felt pain in testing your edges in exercise, as I suggested earlier in the book. Well done. That takes courage. In your business, pain is useful too. Employees complaining about new processes or systems is a symptom of change – usually a sign of growth. Cashflow pain can be a sign of expansion in the business as you reinvest the profits that lead to short-term painful situations. Painful negotiation is often a sign of a genuinely well thought out deal, that has been painstakingly agreed in detail before any contracts have been signed. This attention to detail – for which lawyers are notorious by the way – is often the most effective way to ensure the smooth running of a transaction in the future. It can also save a great deal of pain in the future as it prevents the relationship breaking down when things are not working quite as well as expected or desired. The pain of the sweat equity invested at the beginning saves a whole world of catastrophic pain later on.

The type of pain I am arguing for you to experience in your life, and even (God forbid) perhaps begin to enjoy, is the type of pain we most associate with growing – "Growing Pains" if you like. It is the type of pain most often associated with fear. In other words, you have not actually experienced the pain that you are scared of. It is the fear of the act itself that causes the pain rather than the reality of the pain itself that is causing the concern.

Have you ever walked on fire? I'm not especially into this as a motif myself. I think it's all a bit unnecessary. But I have done it. Many times – mostly as part of various growth and expansion programs I have participated in. I have yet to burn my feet. Why? I put myself in the state that enables my body to undertake the act without the apparent associated consequences. The act of walking on fire is a metaphor for turning fear into power. Thinking about walking on fire is scary. Rationally speaking, I would never, ever do it. And yet, with the support of the right team, and by getting myself into the state of peak performance, then walking on hot coals becomes very possible, easy in fact. That's the benefit of the pain – and the willingness to experience it.

The facing of fear is not the point for you though. The point is this – living on the edge is what you really want in your life. That is necessarily going to involve going to places that you may not otherwise have been before. That's why I am such a big advocate of the practice of yoga. Yoga is uncomfortable — you are seeking to put yourself into positions that stretch you physically... and mentally. The stretch is uncomfortable and unfamiliar. That's the point. Practicing yoga and bringing discipline to your life may involve actions and conversations that stretch you beyond where you have been before. Go there.... You will be glad you did.

CHAPTER TEN

RESTRAINT IS POWER AND CHOICE

Allow Yourself to Get Tied Up

"Restraint" – it is a word filled with meaning and association. We are tuned to think things about it. Whether it's in the bedroom, where you have images of Christian Grey gently caressing you with a leather horsewhip and then beating you with it... all while tied with silk scarves to the bed. Or exercising your restraint, self-will, and discipline in refusing that chocolate soufflé that looks so light and delectable right now, but you know could add inches to your hips overnight, with the light whipped cream and everything else that comes with it. Restraint is tinged with meaning and innuendo that may or may not be real.

Restraint also has a bad rap. We think it is about tying ourselves up – it is; we think it is about surrendering control – it may be; we think it is about depriving ourselves of pleasure and delight – it is not. You probably thought, ouch. This is going to hurt. It may do, but only if you want it to, and you choose for it to do so.

Restraint is actually the thing you have been looking for throughout your life. In other words, restraint is discipline. And discipline is what you want. I have pretty much been saying this all the way through the book. Being disciplined, and being disciplined (think about those phrases, said differently) is the answer all the way along in life. It is quite literally the answer to everything. I know! I hated this concept my whole life, but it is the only thing that I have found that actually did bloody well work!

My mother was first advised by a child psychologist to bring discipline into my life when I was eight – yes, eight years old. I was a willful child, and as an adult, I have remained forthright, quite bolshy, and a bit rebellious. I have an independent streak, and I definitely do not like being told what to do. Discipline has always been a struggle for me, whether I was wanting to exert my own power over myself, or someone else was seeking to discipline me. I resisted big time. How is it possible then that you find yourself reading a book about discipline and its benefits written by yours truly? It is simple, really – being disciplined works.

And I do mean being disciplined in both ways – doing what I promise myself (and it is mostly to myself, we are generally good as a species at keeping our promises to other people but utter rubbish at keeping our promises to ourselves) – like exercising consistently, eating healthy nutritious food, etc. And also doing what someone else asks me and receiving the punishment or correction when I do not perform up to standard. It sounds harsh, and from the external perspective, it might look that way. In my experience, it is not. It is quite life-affirming – I learn where I am weak, which supports me in developing my strengths. I realize quickly when I make mistakes, meaning I can correct them quickly. The key for me is that I am VERY selective about with whom I engage in this activity. Not everyone has my permission. That is fundamental. I have the right to say no, and I frequently do!

I know that we are frequently pumped full of mindless drivel from self-confessed experts that it is all about manifesting and think about what you want – it will happen. I say drivel in a derisory way because while I do believe in the manifesting as a phenomenon, it does not happen on thought alone. Napoleon Hill wrote a book in the 1930s called *Think and Grow Rich*, and ever since, there has been a circus and entertainment industry dressed up as self-improvement that has peddled the notion that *Thoughts Become Things* and if you think of it, it shall be. These experts missed the point of Hill's book. A book that is very thought-provoking and inspiring when you drill down into its key message – be careful what you wish for. Thoughts do indeed become things (I have already written extensively on this subject throughout this book), but they do so because we put energy into those thoughts and actually DO something. DO SOMETHING. There's a concept. That is where the discipline part comes in.

Most of us paint very pretty pictures of how we would like our lives, our intimate connections, and our businesses or careers to be. We might even go so far as to create an inspiring and motivating vision board. But that is about the last thing we actually do. We get supermotivated and inspired – perhaps you went to a workshop or read a book. And then… it's like a car running out of gas; you grind to a halt. Sound familiar? I know it does because it was me. For years. And years. And years. Until I finally learned.

Give my word to myself and stay true to my word. In other words, be disciplined. Create a set of habits and practices that I can live by. Then live by them. I do – it is what I did to write this book. I set myself a goal of writing the first draft during the month of June 2020. I completed the draft on June 24, 2020. I calculated, based on the recommendations of my mentor and coach, that I needed to write 2,000 words a day, five days a week. And I did. I tied myself up – I made myself accountable to myself. I also made myself accountable to my coach and mentor. It worked. I wrote the book.

It is also how I have successfully managed to lose and maintain my weight. I started small. I set myself a target of walking for 45 minutes per day (just walking, no running, no weight training, no yoga, nothing like that) for 120 days. I accomplished that; I then added another 60 days to reach six months and continued. I am at something like 750 days of consistent activity now, as I write this. What did that do for me? I was able to trust that I could and would do what I set out to do and said to myself that I would do. It also provided me with a stable platform on which to build. It was like the bass on the mixing desk that I have casually mentioned throughout the book. It gave me a very solid foundation to be able to start playing about with my body a bit. How come? Because despite exercising consistently over a measurable and sustained amount of time, I did not lose much weight (about 5lbs all in). It was frustrating. And it proved a point to me – losing weight is not about exercise. It is mostly about what I eat.

During this 120-day period, about halfway in, I started to change my eating habits and monitoring my eating with an app called MyFitnessPal. I observed that I was eating about twice as much in calories as I was supposed to. This surprised me, but it also gave me access to another rope with which to bind myself. With the support of the app, and some professional advice, I changed my eating habits and miraculously – while still continuing with the walking – I lost about 15lbs in three weeks. Shocking. But also very useful information. I had started to build the mixing desk I have alluded to.

I was only able to do it, though, because I had paid attention to my habits, monitored their efficacy in producing the results I was seeking, and then changed them when the results were not "manifesting." So yes, I had thought of what I wanted. But then I worked BLOODY hard to make it happen.

Same with being financially free and successful in business. Saying I want to own my own business is a useful starting point, but an entrepreneur it does not make you. An aspirational entrepreneur perhaps, but not an entrepreneur. To be financially free and successful in business, you have to… start the business, and then exercise discipline and rigor in your management of your finances. I'm not especially the person to do this with. I have a funny relationship with money; it works for me and is always available. If you want to learn good money habits and discipline, I have a series of resources that I recommend. I invite you to reach out to me, and we can see which is the most appropriate for you.

So what, you might be muttering to yourself. So what is this? Where are you selling out on yourself? Where are you not willing to put in the work that it takes to dominate in the way that you want to? Where is feeling good and being comfortable more important to you than accomplishing your dream or your desire? Tough questions, I know. But these are the most valuable questions you might ever answer for yourself. These questions will give you the insight and awareness that is at the heart of you dominating your life and business, and orgasm – just as you want to. It's tough, but anything in life that is worth accomplishing generally does take graft and requires hard work. I will say that the awareness of your habits and where you are not living to your own standards is VERY empowering, provided that you do not make yourself wrong and use these realizations as access to self-flagellation. If you want a whipping, have someone else do it for you!

Designing your habits is perhaps the most important step in learning to dominate yourself, and in creating the domination of your life. Up to this point, I have stayed away from this. I don't know about you, but I am fundamentally quite lazy at heart. I would really like nothing more in my life than to lie in bed sleeping for hours, and hours, and hours. Then occasionally waking up, possibly to have sex, eat something, drink something and maybe visit the bathroom. I might watch TV. But that's really about it. The thing is, if I did this, I would be the size of a house or larger, and I would get very bored. Quickly.

Habits maketh the man, so it be said. Woman too, only we weren't given any consideration in the 18th century when this aphorism was coined. But you need to find out what your habits are, as much as any man does! Look at whether the habits you have are working for you or do you need to invest some energy and discipline in cultivating new ones. Trust me when I say cultivate. Habits are like gardening, they take time to bed in. You have to discipline yourself to keep them.

This is where being disciplined (by another) can support you. I hate being accountable to other people. I have already mentioned that I am not good at following direction. Being accountable is a bit like going to prison for me. Actually, being held to account is even worse. I have trained myself to respect and honor my word – because my word matters to me. If I'm honest about it, I could say, I don't really give a f**k about my word to other people. I don't care what other people think of me. Except... that I do. I like to be well thought of. I like to be consistent and reliable. I like to be viewed as trustworthy and a person of high integrity. Being held to account, then, especially when I have fallen short of the mark, is uncomfortable. I am called to face up to my flaws and missteps. I am called to acknowledge where I have made a promise and then not kept it. It is an uncomfortable feeling. But from here, growth comes. From here, I can develop myself in being of service to those I care about, the community more widely, and society at large.

I have to exercise restraint in the process. I have to submit to being disciplined, even by people that I may not have necessarily agreed to disciplining me. The wild, rebellious aspects of my personality resent this. But my commitment to be more than I know myself to be wins the day in the end. Fundamentally that is my point. Submitting yourself to being disciplined by another is an access to power for you that you may not otherwise be able to enjoy. It is the key to dominating your life – in the bedroom, in the boardroom – everywhere. I know. It seems contradictory. It is not.

When we have the courage to acknowledge to ourselves that we do not know everything there is to know in the world; when we are courageous in considering that another's perspective is as valid, if not more so, than our own; in other words, when we submit to another, we create space for people to be free and honest. It is profoundly moving. By the way, I said "we" because I'm talking to myself too. Like I said, this is a tricky one for me. Yet, as Brené Brown has taught, I dare greatly, and in so doing more of life becomes possible, more experiences become available... oh, and my orgasms get that bit louder!

You may want to think about ways to give being disciplined – in both meanings of the phrase – a go. I have given you many opportunities to create new habits and practices for yourself throughout the book – working out, practicing yoga, journaling. You name it, I've given it to you! These are all ways for you to practice being disciplined – for yourself. Being disciplined by others – that is more challenging and, by definition, more exposing. It is, as I have said, the access to power for you. I encourage you to take the risk.

How? Well. Creating promises and accountability relationships is an accessible way to start. For the more courageous of you, I recommend exploring gentle bondage. I do mean gentle. Don't be looking bondage up online – you will scare yourself stupid. Don't be searching for bondage clubs in your neighborhood unless you already frequent them – again, they might mess with your head! Find some silk scarves in your closet, and perhaps encourage your partner to tie you up with them and see where that goes! Or bring food into the equation. Make it easy for yourself. I appreciate exploring yourself and your relationship like this may be new to you. It may feel uncomfortable, and you might feel uneasy. Good. There's growth there. And please look after yourself, take care, and only go where you feel comfortable and safe.

Just so you know, I also have an amazing line of products and locations that can help in this arena. If you want to explore and you want support in doing that, reach out to me. It's what I'm here for – you know the address; I'm not going to give it to you again!!!

CHAPTER ELEVEN

Explore the Push and the Pull

The whole book, up to this point, has been about this subject, in all honesty. Life is all about push and pull. We articulate it in different ways – masculine-feminine; north and south; I call it domination and submission – but you already knew that! Being able to dominate your life and find the discipline you are seeking is really all about being able to find the push and pull in your life.

Sometimes you have to push a boulder up a hill – it requires massive effort, fortitude, and strength of character – it can occur like a force of nature. Sometimes you just move your pinky finger in a certain direction, and the subtlety of the movement creates a whole cascade of motion that is perhaps deeply unexpected but desired. Sometimes you just need to give someone a gentle tug, and the movement occurs, and sometimes, you have to pull the bus. It's not the force of the push or pull that is the point here; it's the direction that matters. And the knowing of which to apply when.

It comes back to the same thing that I have said throughout the book – I'm nothing if not consistent (one of the principles that you need to live by, by the way… being consistent!). The art is in the refinement, and this is where most people go wrong. I've mentioned, a few times through the book, how Michelangelo articulated the carving of David from the slab of marble in front of him. He saw David in the marble and chipped everything away that was not David. Imagine, though, if he had taken a sledgehammer to the piece of marble. No David! And that's what I'm talking about with the push and pull and the art of refinement. Sometimes you need a sledgehammer, but mostly you need a chisel and some tongs.

In the last chapter, I referred to the idea of tying yourself up – I have asked you to give your word to things all the way through this book. I also suggested you might literally want to tie yourself up. The thing is, be careful. Don't tie yourself up so tightly that you can't escape. Even David Blaine, the well-known escapologist, always has an escape route. We may not be able to see it, but it is there. Otherwise, he would not perform the trick (and it is a trick, he is a master of illusion).

So before you do get yourself all tied up in whatever it is that you want to be – whether it be in the bedroom, the boardroom, the basement, the baseball ground (or any other location beginning with "B" or not) you HAVE to consider why you want to be tied up – that is: What are you seeking to accomplish? What is your destination? Where are you going?

Then look at the opportunities, people, places; and resources available to you for fulfillment; getting tied up in bed is very different from getting tied up in a knotty negotiation in the boardroom. You are tied up in both of them, but they have different purposes, mechanisms, and points of access. I would say it is very useful to know which is which before you start – wouldn't you agree?

Finally, consider what you might want to let go of in order to allow for what you are seeking to manifest or be generated in the world – what do you need to get rid of? What do you need to acquire? Who do you want to seek help and support from? All of these are of value to you and deserve some attention and focus.

Focusing in this way is also going to have you see where you need to push – you need to boss people around, dominate yourself and others, get your own house in order. You will also identify where you need to pull, guide, nurture, and perhaps finesse matters at hand, for your fulfillment and orgasm (if you like).

So, go on – take a look, anywhere and everywhere that makes a difference and is of importance to you – *Because you're worth it* ™.

CHAPTER TWELVE

Slow Down and Be Still, Listen to Your Stomach

Does your tummy talk to you? I don't mean growl at you when you haven't eaten that day, or rumble when you have eaten something that does not agree with you. Does your stomach tell you how you feel about stuff that is going on in your life? I alluded to this earlier in the book – do you remember when I was discussing embodiment? Here we are again! You may not be aware of the way that your stomach talks to you; I certainly was not. But yes, scientific evidence now suggests that your tummy is, in fact, very communicative to you!

For about 150 years of scientific research, we have lived under the notion that all human thought occurred in our brains. If you have read any of Freud's seminal work on human psychology and sexuality, then you may be under the impression that all thoughts and feelings flow from our minds, and that our minds reside in our brains.

Esoteric thinking and spirituality have always indicated otherwise. Now science is catching up with that perspective. When I say esoteric thinking, I am referring to the philosophy of yoga, as well as texts that have given rise to the well-known film of the early 2000s, *The Secret*. Esoteric thinking has given us access to understanding ourselves that we in the West have largely ignored for centuries. In the wisdom of the ages, our stomachs and our digestive systems have been great indicators to us of how we feel about things. The sages have taught us to listen to our digestion and the lower parts of our body (from the chin down). Until recently, Western thinking has ignored this.

It is changing now. Science is catching up with the philosophy that has been around for a while. Have you ever heard of something called "Polyvagal theory?" No… I hadn't either. It turns out we have a nerve in our body that extends from the bottom of our skull, through our spine and feeds directly into our digestive system. It is called the vagus nerve. Nothing to do with Las Vegas, as far as I'm aware, but I'm not taking bets on that (geddit…?). This nerve, enervating our stomach, liver, and kidneys – the key organs of our digestive system – has a big part to play in what is now known as our parasympathetic nervous system.

Well, this parasympathetic nervous system of ours is responsible for having us be calm. Our digestive system works most effectively when we are rested, relaxed, and experiencing a sense of well-being. *(Side note – this is critical if you want to lose weight – if you are stressed, it ain't gonna work because our nervous systems won't let it…)* You know, those feelings that you have when life is going well, and you are experiencing all that you want in your life. This is how your stomach feels when all is well, no IBS symptoms, no nasty gas, effortless effort as we say in yoga.

Conversely, when our sympathetic nervous is activated, we are fully immersed in stress, upset, or any other perceived negative experiences we might have in life, then we are enjoying the throes of our fight or flight response in all its amazing physical glory. This is when you may start experiencing IBS symptoms, you might get diarrhea symptoms, or you may become severely constipated. Your stomach is literally telling you THERE IS SOMETHING WRONG HERE. You may also experience less severe symptoms.

Do you see the point? When you are aware of what is going on in your stomach, it tells you something about how you feel in your life and which aspect of your nervous system is at work. Useful tool, huh? So, what is your stomach telling you?

Do you ever meditate? Have you heard of pranayama? I would forgive you if you did not know what pranayama is; it's a curious phenomenon. Pranayama is all about breathing and creating different experiences with breath.

But meditation, meditation is critical. You HAVE to slow down to meditate. If you are not slowing down and stopping to breathe in whatever way works for you, then quite honestly, you are not meditating. Many of the spiritual types that I know swear by meditation – arguing that it has completely saved their lives. I wouldn't say that meditation has saved my life, but it is really helpful. It does give me time to pause, think, and be present to what is going on in my body – which I've already shared with you is a much better barometer for how I'm feeling and what is going on than my head could ever hope to be. How come? Well, simply this, when I meditate, I actually have to sit (or lie, I prefer to lie down when I'm meditating) my ass down and not move. I have to focus on my breathing, and I have to get present. There are lots of different ways to meditate and practice pranayama – I teach some of them on my exclusive retreats – but personally, I find one of the most beneficial ways is to do something called "watching the breath."

It is a simple practice that involves sitting quietly for a defined time period and just breathing. Your action is to focus on your breath and do nothing else. It can be a challenge. Your brain might run a mile. That is the point though. Watching your breath supports discerning the thought patterns that you have that you might want to do something about – you know, those gnarly little beliefs we've talked about before.

Meditation and, in particular, a breath meditation, like watching your breath, is also really good for your health (and might help you lose weight and feel better). It supports more oxygen coming into your lungs. It slows down your heart rate because you are sitting quietly, your cortisol levels can reduce, and your parasympathetic nervous system goes to work.

If you want to learn more about how to meditate and watch your breath, there are some videos on my website, www.suzannepool.com and if you would really like to learn properly, then drop me a line to helpcoachmenow. suzannepool.com indicating that you would like to know more about my retreats, and we can practice together.

Now it's time for a short anatomy lesson. I'm a trained yoga teacher, not a doctor, so please forgive the brevity. But I do have a vague interest in anatomy and how to empower people to make better decisions for themselves.

The thing is though, most of us are moving way too quickly through life to even notice that our stomachs and bodies are talking to us. Slow the fuck down! If you were a hippy in the 1960s, I would tell you to go smell the daisies. But we're living in the 21st century, and even when we're stuck at home, locked in because of a rogue microbe, it's still like you're driving on the freeway (motorway as we say in the U.K.). Speeding to who the fuck knows where.

Have you ever driven through Los Angeles? It's a funny place to drive. You HAVE to have a car when you are there because it is a monster of a sprawling metropolis – spreading more than 50 miles in diameter in all directions. LA has a network of freeways that worm their way through the city. I say worm because that is what the freeways are like, they move very slowly and almost grind their way through. Frequently, it is quicker to take what is known as the surface streets – you know the ones, with stop signs, traffic lights, and lots of turns. It seems contrary, but sometimes the slow way is quicker, even Google maps says so. Remember the Aesop's Fable of your childhood – the tortoise and the hare? Which one won the race? Oh, yes, the tortoise. So slow down and start noticing what your body is telling you.

Slowing down is really useful for many other reasons too. It will help your heart and your lungs – I already went into that with you when I wrote about meditation. It will also help in the discernment piece that I spoke of earlier. You might start to identify what matters to you. I've already shared at length with you about how important it is for you to be clear about what matters to you. Here's another reason why finding out what matters to you is helpful. Have you heard of leverage? People often talk about leverage in relation to property and running businesses – how can you leverage the support of other people and their money?

I'm asking you to look at what matters to you and what doesn't. Then perhaps you can leverage people around you to do what you find less than thrilling. For me, this is about cleaning. I hate cleaning. I wish I were Monica from *Friends*, getting a thrill out of donning my rubber gloves and scrubbing. Honestly, the COVID-19 lockdown has taught me that I just never am going to be like that. I simply hate cleaning. As soon as I was permitted to by the U.K. government, I brought my cleaners back into my home, and thank God. I was literally losing my mind. I leverage cleaning my home as soon as I possibly can.

In your journal, write a list of things that you need to take care of in your life that you would love to clear out of your life. Now write another list of people and resources that you have available to you, that you could ask for help in relation to the first list. And get to it! You can only do this, though, when you slow down and get present to what you have in your life that you want to get rid of.

The final key benefit of slowing down is that you can begin to undertake your actions deliberately. I have casually mentioned this all the way through this book, but up to now, I have not really articulated it fully. What does it mean to do things deliberately? It means that you have stopped to consider the appropriateness of your proposed course of action. You have given time to think about what is important to you about what it is that you are dealing with. You have given due care and attention to the relationships that matter to you.

We have already invested a fair amount of time in having you investigate this for yourself. And you have done that work. I know you have, or you would not be this far into reading the book! When you work deliberately and take the time to assess your course of action, and then assess the efficacy of your results, you move the mixing desk more effectively. You begin to see which levels have more impact on the results you are seeking in your life. You can also give yourself the time to generate the courage that you need to step into action, a conversation, or a project that looks uncomfortable or challenging.

Have you ever seen *Indiana Jones and the Temple of Doom?* There's a moment toward the end of the movie when the Indy character is hiding on a ledge with a deep cavern between him and his quarry. He knows that he needs to get to the other side, and he needs to get there quickly. It looks hopeless. There is no way across. He considers his options, and finally grabs some of the sand that is surrounding his hiding place. He tosses the sand across the cavern, and miraculously stones appear. They had been hidden prior to that. Indy had to deliberate on what to do before the stones could appear. He also had to trust the process and go for it! He threw the sand, and the stones showed up.

Where can you see that this applies to your life? Where do you need to find the courage to deliberate and then take action in your life to dominate the area you want, or to find your discipline? I'd love to hear – head over to all-eyes.suzannepool.com and let me know! Truly – I want to know!

CHAPTER THIRTEEN

TELL YOUR BOSS, CLIENTS, OR HUSBAND TO SHOVE IT

You might think I have been building up to this for the entire book. You would be wrong. It might seem that I have been drawing you to a point where you are getting ready to write (or may even have written) your resignation letter. It might seem like I have been drawing you to the conversation for divorce with your husband – or perhaps you have already done that. I have to tell you I AM NOT SAYING DO ANY OF THOSE THINGS. In fact, if you followed my advice in the Introduction to this book, then I know that you most certainly have NOT taken any of those actions. And for that, I say, well done. It is fair to say though, that this chapter is due and that having read this far, you are ready to read what I have to say now.

I know the message of this book is take control of your life and dominate wherever you choose to. I trust by now that you have realized that my understanding of domination is not the common, out in the world, understanding of domination. I'm pretty sure that you have realized that my exposition of domination is based on an examination of what it is that you want in your life, in your bedroom, in your relationships, in your career and in your business. My exposition of domination is based on knowing your boundaries and knowing how and when to enforce your boundaries with other people. It is based on knowing when you need to work hard, and at what you have to work hard (be disciplined). And it is based on knowing when it is to your benefit to cede control and power to a third party (be disciplined). You might then realize that telling your boss, clients, or whomever you want to "SHOVE IT" is not the point. It isn't. And it might be.

This is the paradox of life. Sometimes standing up for yourself and fighting for what you believe, or even your right to party, is the right way to go. Go ahead – dominate the fuck out of whatever it is that is pissing you off, shout from the rooftops and do whatever it takes. Sometimes though, it is way more appropriate to address the situation you are facing with honey. To submit. To allow. To receive. To cede the power. To accept that you do not have all the answers. Your key to being able to dominate your life as I know that you want to is to understand the difference for you and to know which form of discipline to apply, and when. This is true power and does not involve any force at all – the form of power we typically understand in the world. In this power, you might choose to find yourself a new boss (or manager I prefer), or you might choose to have a conversation with your existing manager. You might also choose to let some (or all) of your current clients go, or you might choose to transform the conversation with your clients into one that has never existed before.

This paradox of controlling and allowing is the ultimate purpose of this book. We've been looking at it mostly through the lens of your personal life up to this point. Let's have a look at it through your professional life now. I don't know whether you have your own business, or you have a high-powered career. What I do know about you is that you are ambitious, and you want more for yourself in your life. If that weren't you, you wouldn't be reading this book, and you definitely would not have gotten yourself all the way to Chapter Thirteen.

Inside of that ambition, you may or may not have been deliberate. You may or may not have been disciplined. You may or may not have had a plan that you have executed. It doesn't matter. Whatever the history, from this point forward, this much is true: You will have a plan that you execute. You will be disciplined, and you will be deliberate. I know that because I said so!

Whether you are career-minded and are seeking to be the best that you can be in the profession you are blessed with, or you are entrepreneurial and have your own business or businesses, you must remember that at the core of it all is

YOU. What do I mean by that? You have the choice in the ties that bind you. I realized this one for myself.

I trained as a lawyer, and to be honest, I fell into that career by accident, but also by intention. I knew that I wanted to work in the music business, and in particular, I was very keen to understand the relationship between music and commerce – I wanted to understand THE BUSINESS of making music, I was never interested in the creative aspects.

That said, I graduated from university with no job, and honestly, no clear idea of where I wanted to dedicate my energy. I went to Law School. It was an easy option for me. I got to live with my parents (cheaper), live in London, which I was desperate to do, and continue being a student – with the fun and limited responsibility that comes with student life. For me, going to Law School was an easy and fun option. I did not really think too much beyond the end of my nose, let alone about what was going to happen in the future.

More fool me! I arrived at Law School with no clear pathway other than oh, I think it would be fun to work in the music industry. I had no clarity about what I was going to learn while I was in Law School, what the course involved, or how much work it was going to take. And it took A LOT of work. Now don't get me wrong, I succeeded at Law School, I trained as an attorney with a boutique media and music firm in London, and within less than one year of qualifying and being licensed as an attorney, I was hired by one of the major record labels in London to work direct with the artists and producers. It was the stuff of dreams. I was invited to lots of cool parties. I hung out with famous artistes. But… I hated it.

Really, I was just a glorified paper pusher. I had sworn all my adolescent years that the one thing I would never be was a paper pusher. And yet, what did I do – admin. Yes, I was qualified as a lawyer, but the job was quite administrative, sexy administration maybe, but administration nevertheless. If I had done some research before embarking headlong into this career path, I might have realized it was not for me and saved myself about a decade of anguish.

That was a long story for a short point! You don't have time to waste doing things that you don't want to. You don't have resources to invest in finding out what you want to be bound and tied to. You need to be assured that you are making a good choice for you when you are ready to commit. How do you do that? You put the time in up front, that's how. You do the research, you consider, you do your due diligence – before you say YES. Once you've gotten into the commitment, it's really too late to back out.

What does that mean in your business? It means you have to engage your brain. You have to think about what it is that you want (there it is again). You have to check the references. You have to do the due diligence and find out about the people you are negotiating with. You have to consider your resources. You have to consider your strategies and actions. You have to consider your opportunities. You have to consider your teammates and your employees.

Yes, there is a lot to consider. Yes, it does take effort and energy. But when you have done this work, and then you commit – you are committed because you exercised your choice and power. You did the work; you considered the options, and you chose. You are committed, not obligated. Energetically it is an entirely different experience in which to engage in a transaction, a role, or any other type of business arrangement. Try it – you'll see what I mean.

A sense of obligation arises out of a feeling of "have to." It is connected to subjugation and being victimized. You are acting out of compulsion not choice or free will. There is little power in acting anywhere in life from feeling obligated, and most definitely, that is the case in business. Take a look at your job for a moment – how inspiring and enthralling is it to get up in the morning when you feel like you "have to" do that? I remember those days. I would usually wait until the very latest possible moment to get up for work, leave the house in a rush, unkempt, and unprepared for the day ahead. I would grin and bear the horror that is the London Underground network in rush hour (it's like herding cattle, everyone crammed in small, dark, airless trains), and then I would arrive at work disheveled and very (very) grumpy. *Working Girl* – that movie from the 1980s with Melanie Griffith and Harrison Ford, it most definitely was not.

Can you see where you are operating your business, managing your team, or going to work each day operating from a place of obligation? How does it make you feel? How do you feel about doing your job each day? How exhausted are you when you get home every night? Is your weekday to weekday existence pretty much like this?

Get up, get dressed, go to work, work, work, work, come home, have dinner, watch TV, go to sleep – rinse and repeat? Make a note in your journal of how reading this is leaving you feeling. We're going to come back to that.

When you engage with your ambition and your deliberation, you start to see what is available to you from different perspectives. Your level of ownership of the games you are engaged in starts to alter, and I say elevate. You become willing to take responsibility where you were unwilling before. You begin to take risks that you did not know were even available to you, let alone that you might now contemplate. You begin to ask for what it is that you want to happen. In short, you can start to dominate your business, your career, and your life.

You also create a space in which you can allow and have people be free. You become better able to express yourself, and others have greater permission to express themselves. You will start to experience freedom, and hopefully, fun in ways you never imagined were possible. But this only comes about when you think deliberately and move in carefully constructed ways.

The balance is a tricky one. We tend to move through life either half asleep (sometimes not even half!) or like bulldozers churning through everything in our path. You may remember earlier on in the book I talked about the Godzilla tail, that's what I mean. When you wake up from the dozy state you have probably been in all your life, the temptation is very great to swing the pendulum very far the other way. This scares people. Trust me, I know. I've been there. It alarms them to see this very sudden (for them) change in behavior. You may be aware of all that has preceded it. The enormous work that you have put in. But most people will not appreciate the journey you have been on and the path that you have trodden. It is important, and even imperative, that you be mindful of other people in this waking up phase. The deliberation and consideration are even more important for them than they are for you. Pay attention!

And now back to whether you are going to tell your boss or your clients... to shove it. Have you got all your ducks in a row? Do you know what I mean when I say that? Probably not. Again, I didn't for a long time. I had a vague sense of what I wanted, but no clear idea of what that really meant. If there is one thing that I have learned over the years of being in commercial life, whether in corporate or as an entrepreneur, it is this: Have a plan. Be ready to rip the plan up, because it will go the way of the gods almost as soon as you embark on the journey. But have a plan. If you do not, you will never know where you are going (remember my fixation with knowing where you are aiming for?), you will not realize when you get there, and you will not be able to course-correct if you lose sight of the shore. Knowing your destination is vital, and is without a doubt the first duck to line up.

What assets do you have control over? Notice how deliberate I have been in my choice of words here.

When we usually discuss assets, it is all about ownership, ownership, ownership. It does not need to be. Controlling assets is just as useful as owning them. Do you even know what an asset is? Is the home you live in, if you own it, an asset or a liability? (Answer at the end of the chapter…) What is the most important asset you have in your life? (Clue – you're much closer to this than you realize…) It is vital that we know what assets we have available to us in the pursuit of our objectives in life. It is also vital that we know what assets we have control over and those that we need to move to access. This is the second duck you need to get in a row. When you are fully present to the assets that you have control over and access to, you can start to look at the most effective and efficient way to accomplish your objectives and goals. This is the case whether you are in business for yourself or climbing the career ladder.

By the way – on the question of what the most important asset that you have available to you and that you have control over, the clue is in the question. The answer is YOU. You have the ability to direct how you operate, with whom you interact, and the ways that you do so. You are the most important asset that you have available to you. So, let's do an inventory now of your assets, including yourself, and also the networks that you have access to, or desire to become part of. These are all assets that can and will support you in accomplishing your objectives in life and dominating your business and career in the way that had you pick up this book!

There are other smaller ducks that you will want to get in a row if you are in business or you have a project to manage, your career, or any aspect of your life really. I am not going to go into what they all are; if I did that, we would literally never finish! If you are interested in knowing more about the ducks, then why don't you reach out to me? You know I love to hear from you! And just as a reminder, you can contact me at all-eyes.suzannepool.com

So let me be clear, once and for all, before we move on: whatever the move you decide to make in your life, it is important (that's an understatement) that you know why you want to make that move, what your intention is for your life, and what you are seeking to accomplish. Do not read that like it is designed to stop you – you do have to make the move, and you do have to make the jump. But the point is this, don't just tell people to F* the f*** off, without good reason. It needs to be in your best interests, in concern for you, and be of service to them too. But if, after deliberation and consideration, you realize that the best course of action is to tell them to step off and step away, then DO IT! And more power to you. Here endeth the lesson…

Answer to the earlier question – is the home you live in (if you own it) an asset or a liability?

It's a liability. It costs you money to live in it, even if you own it outright – there are bills to pay to maintain the property. It's a liability.

CHAPTER FOURTEEN

You Must Pay Attention to What You Say

I have been saying this all the way through this book. But now it is time to say it in a complete chapter and right at the end of the book, no less!! Be careful what you wish for. And in particular, be careful what you wish for... out loud. Your words create the world. Huh? I struggled with this notion for a VERY long time. The level of responsibility that comes with the realization that your words create the world is really awe-inspiring. If you are not careful, it can feel like you are Atlas carrying the weight of the world on your shoulders. And yet, it is super empowering when you realize what becomes possible if and when you accept the notion that what you say does, in fact, create the world.

Nelson Mandela is famous for having said at his inauguration, "Our deepest fear is not that we are inadequate. Our deepest fear is that we are powerful beyond measure. It is our light, not our darkness that most frightens us."

It was not actually Nelson Mandela who wrote this. It's a quote from a famous 1970s spiritual work *A Return to Love* by Marianne Williamson. The point of the quote remains the same 50 years later and is the reason Mandela quoted it in 1993. Our power and ability to create what we want in the world can be overwhelming. It is this power that arises when we realize that we create the world with our words. As Yoda said to a young Jedi, Luke Skywalker, *"the Force is strong in this one."*

Our words have the power to lift people up, to lift ourselves up, and to enable others we are not connected to rise up and move past their circumstances. Think of the powerful rhetoric of Mahatma Gandhi or Martin Luther King Jr in the mid 20th century; these men caused generations of people to bind together to overcome their oppressors and create new levels of freedom in their respective societies. Our words can also impact others to create hate and division; our current crop of politicians (in 2020), sadly, are particularly effective at the use of divisive language and rhetoric.

Do you remember the Ice Bucket Challenge that took hold on Facebook and other social media platforms during the summer of 2014? It was a strange phenomenon that could only have become possible with the galvanizing force of social media that has taken a vicelike grip of our relationships and lives in the early part of the 21ˢᵗ century. The main crux of the challenge was that a person was challenged, by a "friend" on Facebook to dump a bucket of ice (a large bucket, not a genteel bucket that you might chill a bottle of wine in, but more like a large trashcan) over your own head, record this process happening on video and then post said video of such episode to your Facebook profile. If you declined to do so, you were invited to send a donation to an American charity associated with the challenge. The challenge was MASSIVE, it was literally all people were talking about during the summer of 2014, and it was pretty much all that was on my Facebook feed for months, and months… and well… months.

So what? What's my point here? Good question – this movement, that's what it was, only became possible through the power of language. People were galvanized into action by the call to participate, and through social proof and engagement (also phenomena of language), they were almost shamed into participating in this strange activity. What you don't realize is that the charity associated with the Ice Bucket Challenge raised about 25 times more in funds during the 2014 fundraising cycle than it had previously done (ever) and has done since. This is the power of language and words at work.

Words have the power to move us, to galvanize us, and to destroy us. I say it again – be careful what you say out loud. Your words leave an impression on other people, but mostly on you. Your unconscious mind pays attention to what it is that you say. So if you say, "I'm always late" your unconscious mind will begin to program itself to have you fulfill on that; your mind operates in the pattern that what you say must be true and that what you speak is an order (like in a restaurant). "I'm always late" translates into a pattern of behavior called lateness. What? You're not serious – surely, I was late as a pattern of behavior and then I started saying, "I'm always late." You're thinking that to yourself, aren't you? Yes… see?

That's how predictable we are as humans. I can literally write a sentence in the book, and I will know what response it is going to provoke in you as you read! By the way – this is what advertisers, and entertainers, and politicians, and almost everyone that is seeking to influence you is doing ALL THE TIME! They are choosing their words, very deliberately, to ensure that you provide a certain response – renowned psychologist and author of various books on influence – Robert Cialdini – calls this *"Click Whirr."*

Anyway, back to the "I'm always late" scenario. It's curious, right? Which came first: the pattern of behavior called being late or the belief "I'm always late". The truth is that they arise almost simultaneously. We are late, then we start telling ourselves we are always late, and so we are perpetually late. This, by the way, is how those gnarly limiting beliefs arise as patterns; they start when we are very young, perhaps before we can even walk and talk. It takes deliberate effort and consistent practice to break yourself of the habit of being late, as well as to break yourself of the habitual thinking "I'm always late." You have been doing that work all the way through this book, but now you understand a bit more about why. By the way, I can testify to how much of a struggle these habitual patterns of behavior and thinking are to break. I have already shared with you about my own struggle with weight. I had to break binge-eating and compulsive-eating habits. It was a long hard slog, but it is why I am qualified to write the words you are reading now. And breaking those habitual patterns took changing the way that I spoke with myself and spoke out loud. I had to pay attention (greatly) to the language and words that I was using.

When you are truly aware of the power of your words, then you start to realize the power that you have in the world. You are able to influence and impact people at levels that you did not know was possible. Before I wrote this book, I did not know that I had this book in me. And yet there are words on the page, and you are reading them! And as you have read, I have asked you to engage in different types of activities and exercises. I have influenced you to take different actions. That is the power of words in action.

Let's have a look at your top 100 experiences that you created way back in Chapter One of the book, and while you are at it, let's have another look at your code of conduct and ethics as well. Have you got them? Good. I know you have already done this exercise, but we're going to do it again. Now that you have gone into why pain is actually good for you, you know more about slowing down and being deliberate, this activity is going to take on a whole new meaning for you. What can you see? What do you notice? What do you hear when you speak the goals and experiences out loud? How about the code? Does it move you? Now most important, what do you feel? What is your vision? Are these experiences and this code calling you fully into the world and into your life? YES!!! AMAZING! No. OK, good to notice, let's do some work again then. And by the way, if the answer is yes, you still want to do this work again, as there is always room for improvement. So, come on… Let's do this – let's move you, let's inspire you, and let's call you MASSIVELY into being in the world with your words!

You know I am almost fanatical about knowing where it is that you are going. That is pretty much a theme of EVERY single chapter I have already shared. Have you considered why? It's like this really: if you are on a flight from Los Angeles to New York, and the pilot sets the autopilot one degree off to the south of New York for the duration of the flight, do you know where that flight would end up? In Miami…! that's where. One thousand miles south of its intended destination. Not good, right? You bet your ass… Just one degree for 3,000 plus miles, and you end up way off course. This is why it is so important to set yourself up to WIN! Knowing where you are going, by powerfully engaging with yourself and the world, is going to make a MASSIVE difference in you accomplishing your dreams, fulfilling your potential, and dominating your life in the bedroom, boardroom, and everywhere beyond.

Yet again, I'm going to say that knowing where you are going is probably the most critical element that you can manage. You can determine what matters to you. You can determine where you want to invest your energy and resources. You can determine what is OK for you and what is not. Remember a couple of chapters back when I shared with you that pain is actually an opportunity for you to explore your edges and your boundaries? That is what I am talking about. YOU get to say what matters most to you. Once, that is, you have given up any stories and past behaviors that you might have about being a victim and being put upon. I am trusting that you are far enough into this book to know that those stories are LIES that you have been told, or been telling yourself, to make things seem easier. They are NOT true. And they prevent you from getting yourself on the path that most matters to you. So, let's have another look at that code of conduct and ethics. Let's take another cruise around your values and beliefs. And let's construct language that moves you to tears, that has you singing from the rafters and that galvanizes you into action.

CLOSING THOUGHTS

If I were to sum up the entire point of my message to you, I would do so in four sentences. And while I'm about it – why don't I?

1. Choose your tugs of war – in other words, choose what matters to you, and choose the battles that you fight for. Choose what you commit to. Choose the direction you want to go in. Sound familiar? LOL – as I've said, I'm nothing if not consistent!

2. Find your mixing desk – work out what the levers of change and transformation are for you; this takes paying attention and measuring things.

3. Measure what matters – if you don't you won't be able to be the sound engineer that your life requires for you to dominate in the way that you are seeking.

4. Negotiating life, love and all things in between is a matter of give and take, push and pull, giving and receiving.

That's it – four simple sentences. Has it been worth it? Have I given you something to think about and consider? I think I have. I am going to go into a final push on detail, just for the sake of it, but I know that you have gotten the hang of this by now. And if you haven't, then reach out to me – help!menow.suzannepool.com with the subject line – I NEED YOUR HELP. And I will know what you mean. Asking for help, by the way, is the single biggest act of compassion and courage for yourself that you can take in creating your life in the way that you are seeking.

Back to the detail… You need to choose your tugs of war. Choose the battles that you fight for. Where are you going to devote your time and your energy? Where do you want to commit your resources, your time and attention? Your resources, time, and energy are yours to invest and utilize as you can determine – YOU ARE FREE. You can choose where, when, and how you want to dominate – whether it be yourself or other people. (Although if you are choosing to dominate others, then you do need to pay attention to the following: Do you have their permission to dominate those people? Do you know what the boundaries are of the domination? In other words – BE MINDFUL and BE RESPECTFUL; people deserve to be granted the same permissions and freedoms that you are seeking for yourself.) But if you want to take control of your life – everywhere – you need to be aware of where and when you want that control and how to manage it effectively. It is the MOST fundamental point.

Here are some ways to start this process:

1. De-clutter – all over the place. Clutter is like fat – it covers up the beauty of the work of art – think of it like the marble slab with the David statue in it. Remember that example? I shared it with you much earlier in the book, more than once. Michelangelo is reported to have described the process of carving the statue of David as removing all the marble that was superfluous to the statute. David was inside

the marble all the time – Michelangelo's job as the sculptor was to remove all the excess baggage.

2. Envision your masterpiece – it takes planning to create a masterpiece. You have to know where it is that you're going. Michelangelo could see the image of David inside the marble – he had a clear picture in his mind. I could give you many (many) more metaphors here, but you get the point – where, how, and what do you want to dominate? What do you want to create? WHAT ARE YOU UP TO?

3. Consider what is OK for you and what is not. What are your boundaries? What are your limits? What are you putting up with?

It mostly comes down to the questions that you are asking yourself. Are the questions that you are asking yourself empowering you? Are they supporting your growth and development? Are they encouraging you to explore what is possible for you? The questions that you ask yourself will determine what you choose to dominate and how you choose to dominate it. Pay attention to the questions you are asking yourself!

You know I am fanatical about measuring. Measuring what matters to you is the access to creating transformation and change in your life. If you don't measure, you will never know where you are. You have to start this journey where you are. Much as we would love to start the journey where you want to get to, if you think about it, it is quite a logical fallacy – you are where you are! Start there... Does it make sense to go from Charing Cross to Edinburgh if you are starting in New York? Probably not! You have to get to Charing Cross first. So start where you are.

What does that mean in this context? When you consider what it is that you want to measure, think of why you want to measure that thing. Here's a very concrete example for you – you want to lose weight. I have already urged you – greatly – to create a powerful, positive intention for your weight loss. Most of us embark on a weight loss journey in a vague sense of self-disgust. We don't like the way that we look. We are upset about the fact that walking upstairs has become challenging. Creating weight loss from here doesn't work. I know, I've tried it, hundreds (and possibly thousands) of times, since I was 14 years old. You have to have a positive intent for weight loss, or you won't take the VERY deliberate and consistent actions that a successful weight loss program requires. You might tend toward a quick fix. Again – it won't work, and it definitely won't be sustainable in the long term.

Creating a positive vision for yourself, a positive outcome, perhaps a picture of how you want to look when you have successfully lost the weight will help you on the journey. Although to be fair, the biggest thing that you can do for yourself in a weight loss journey is to learn to love yourself just as you are and perhaps to acknowledge that you don't even need to lose weight at all (who knew?! Ha Ha!).

Now back to the measures – so you have set yourself a goal to lose weight, and your mission is positively intended. You have clear outcomes for yourself. Now you got to find out where you are! Go on then, weigh yourself. Measure yourself. Find out what your numbers are. This is where you are starting. It's helpful to know where you are, right? OK good, now those things that you are going to measure make more sense because you have a context – and you have a destination toward which you are heading, and a port from where to start.

As you have now embarked on the journey – you have left port, you have found out where you are, and started taking the actions you determined in the early part of the process. Now you have your mixing desk! You can become your own sound engineer. With the metrics that you are measuring, you can start to tweak the knobs (so to speak) and move the levels. This is power – you have the ability to move and control your life and your accomplishments as you determine. PROVIDED YOU PAY ATTENTION – burying your head in the sand will not get you anywhere.

This is really it. Of course, there's more to it than I have summarized in this final chapter, but trust me, you have enough here to dominate any area of your life. Remember to pay attention, and if you are confused or feel like you would like someone to guide you along the way, then reach out to me help!coachmenow.suzannepool.com. And most important – please let me know how you get on and all about your successes! all-eyes.suzannepool.com

Lots of love and screaming orgasms

Suzanne xx

Recommended Reading

Honestly, I could go on forever here; there are so many books, podcasts, and audiobooks that I would recommend.

But if I were to pick one, I would start with *The Artist's Way* by Julia Cameron.

After that, I invite you to reach out to me, and I can send you my list, or we can talk, and I can find out more about you and make some recommendations that way.

all-eyes.suzannepool.com

That's it, really.

ABOUT THE AUTHOR

Photo © 2020 Becky Rui

Having broken through her own barren, celibate, career-dominated life of her 30s to living a fulfilling, adventurous, and seriously fun (in all ways!) life in her 40s, Suzanne now works as an award-winning Women's Sexual Empowerment Coach. She typically works with women in their 40s, 50s, and beyond, coaching from a place where all dreams are possible, and the only thing preventing them from materializing is the unseen.

Suzanne uses an eclectic mix of hypnosis, NLP, conversational coaching, yoga, and other physical activity to support her clients in discovering who they are and creating the relationships in all areas of life that they are seeking.

Suzanne has consistently shown her clients that it is possible to grasp life by the horns, conquer their fears, and live life as a daring adventure – no matter their age or where they live in the world.

Prior to her coaching and consulting work, Suzanne graduated from Cambridge University with a degree in History and was a successful Business Affairs Manager and lawyer in the media industry, drawing on two decades of experience. During this time, she had the pleasure of working with some of the largest and smallest media companies, rights owners, and intellectual property businesses, both in the U.K. and internationally. Her experience spanned the games, TV, music, and movie sectors. Suzanne always possessed a natural flair for management and leadership.